SPELLING

AN OVERVIEW OF

RESEARCH &

CURRENT RESEARCH

INFORMATION

AND PRACTICES

ScottForesman

A Division of HarperCollins*Publishers*

Editorial Offices: Glenview, Illinois
Regional Offices: Sunnyvale, California • Tucker, Georgia
Glenview, Illinois • Oakland, New Jersey • Dallas, Texas

ISBN 0-673-28840-4

Table of Contents

What About Spelling?

Questions Teachers Are Asking
Answers from Current Research

1. Should I teach spelling?

Yes. Spelling cannot be left to chance. It is true of course that allowing students to invent their own spelling, particularly in the early elementary grades, results in higher achievement in spelling (Cramer, 1967; Stauffer and Hammond, 1969). However, a well-planned spelling curriculum is a major factor in producing better spellers. Students need to be taught basic spelling patterns of words, selected generalizations about spelling, and specific strategies that competent spellers use, as well as strategies for proofreading for spelling and developing an appreciation for competent spelling (Henderson, 1985; Thomas, 1979; Gentry and Gillet, 1993). To relegate spelling instruction to incidental occurrences sends a message to students that spelling really isn't very important. Most students simply will not realize their potential as spellers unless spelling is taught on a sustained basis along with their daily writing activities.

2. Should spelling words be taken from what students are reading?

It is most important that words students are asked to study for spelling are words they commonly use in writing. Extensive samples of children's writing provide a base for spelling instruction (Gentry and Gillet, 1993; Cramer and Cipielewski, 1995). In many cases the words students are reading are also the words they are writing. When students see an interesting or unusual spelling pattern in a word they are reading, it may be appropriate to discuss the spelling pattern of the word in the context of a reading situation.

Reading vocabulary may be used in spelling instruction, as long as the words are developmentally appropriate (according to the child's developmental spelling stage) and are presented with other words with a similar spelling pattern or feature.

3. Just what words should students be learning to spell?

Building valid spelling lists is the most difficult task in developing an effective spelling curriculum. List building requires a thorough acquaintance with research on word frequency, spelling error patterns, the developmental stages of spelling, and letter-sound correspondences. In developing spelling lists, first of all, one must be very sensitive to the selection of words. Words used must be in the students' speaking and writing vocabulary and must be words students at a particular age or grade level are likely to use frequently in their daily language activities (Cramer, 1995). Second, children should have continuous and repeated exposure across grade levels to words that research tells us are the most difficult to learn. Third, children should learn words that are most relevant to their daily work in school—content words in fields of study such as social studies, health, science, reading, and math. Fourth, children should learn words that are appropriate for their stage of development in word knowledge, particularly their understanding of the phonemic, structural, and meaning features of words.

Fifth, word lists should be organized so that exposure to words occurs over a period of years from first through high school grade levels. (Cramer and Cipielewski, 1995; Hanna, Hanna, Hodges and Rudorf, 1966; Venesky and Weir, 1966; Gates, 1936)

4. What is the most effective way to present spelling words?

Spelling words should be presented in a form that helps students understand spelling generalizations. For this reason, it is desirable to present spelling words in a list. Students need to see words in patterns as in *could, would,* and *should* or *weigh, sleigh, eight,* and *neighbor.* In this form students can make generalizations about spelling (Henderson, 1985; Thomas, 1979; Gentry and Gillet, 1993). Words should also be presented to demonstrate a contrasting pattern, for example, words that have short and long vowels. By contrasting certain spelling patterns, students can more easily learn what features go with what words. Words act as exemplars for students to see patterns among words and develop reasonable generalizations for spelling additional words in the future.

5. What is the single most effective technique in learning to spell?

The proper use of a pretest can be the single most effective technique for learning to spell. A pretest is a metacognitive strategy— a way of monitoring and controlling one's own understanding or lack of it. Metacognitive spelling strategies build awareness of the words one knows, doesn't know, or may be uncertain about. Good spellers usually know if a word they've spelled is right or wrong, whereas poor spellers usually do not. A promising way to improve spelling achievement of both good and poor spellers, therefore, is to teach them to evaluate and correct their own spelling performance. When administered properly, a pretest enables students to diagnose and correct their own spelling errors. Graham and Miller (1982) put the case for self-correction like this: "The single most effective technique in learning to spell is followed when the student (under the teacher's direction) corrects his or her own errors immediately after taking a spelling test. The corrected-test method allows the student to (a) see which words are difficult, (b) locate the part of the word that is troublesome, and (c) correct errors" (p. 309). Research on spelling, metacognition, and self-monitoring strategies supports this position (Brown and Palinscar, 1982; Horn, E., 1960; Horn, T., 1947; Moffett and Wagner, 1976).

6. Are there common types of spelling errors that students make repeatedly?

Yes. The Research in Action project found both specific and general error patterns in spelling. These error patterns are spelled out in detail in "Research in Action: A Study of Spelling Errors in 18,599 Written Compositions of Children in Grades 1–8" by Cramer and Cipielewski (1995). Three of the key error patterns are:

1. *Word frequency errors:* A small set of common words tend to be misspelled over and over. These words are misspelled by students at primary, intermediate, and middle school levels.
2. *Homophone errors:* Overall, homophones are the second most common spelling error, and the percentage of homophone errors increases across grade levels. Usage errors are a particular problem when spelling homophones.
3. *Orthographic errors:* Omitted letters, substituting one consonant for another, scrambled letters, schwa-vowel errors, long and short *e* errors, consonant blends, and compound word errors rank among the most frequent spelling errors across grade levels 1–8 (Cramer and Cipielewski, 1995).

7. What is the place of writing in spelling instruction?

Writing must occupy a prominent place in learning to spell. Unless writing is a frequent and significant part of classroom instruction, children will have difficulty learning the mechanics of writing, particularly spelling. Writing serves two important roles in spelling instruction. One is to provide opportunities to use words that have been or are being learned. With frequent writing, the spelling of these words becomes more a motor response than a cognitive one. The other role is to allow students to apply what they know to words that they want to write but don't know how to spell. Some call this invented spelling because students use what they know to invent or approximate the word they wish to write. This testing ground for spelling is important for teachers because it provides insight into what spelling stage primary students are in and what they know about words that they misspell (Beers and Beers, 1991; Calkins, 1986; Clark, 1989; Graves, 1983; Cramer, 1970; Stauffer and Hammond, 1965).

8. Should I teach words from the content areas in my spelling program?

It is appropriate to teach content words in a spelling program. These words are relevant because they are words students are encountering as they read and write about the topics they are learning about in subject areas such as science, health, social studies, geography, and so on. (Gentry and Gillet, 1993). When choosing content area words to use, it is best to select the words that are most commonly used in the particular content area at your grade level. It is also important to consider words that are commonly used in contexts other than just the content areas. For example, words such as *emergency, balance,* and *volume* not only have specific meanings in health, science, and math, but also are widely used in other contexts. It is most appropriate to first approach content words as vocabulary words. Once children know the meanings of the words and how to use them, content area vocabulary could be combined with words with similar spelling patterns and taught as spelling words.

9. What are spelling strategies and how do you teach them?

Spelling strategies are practical, workable plans for helping children learn unfamiliar words. Strategies also help students remember how to spell words that are difficult for them. Some of the most commonly used strategies are visualizing, pronouncing words carefully, matching words with similar spelling patterns, and using meaning-related words (Thomas, 1979; Henderson, 1985; Gentry and Gillet, 1993). Teachers and students should work together to make students aware of their strengths and needs as spellers and to determine which strategies each student needs to apply. Unfamiliar and difficult words can impede the free flow of ideas onto paper. As students internalize spelling strategies over time, they will write more fluently as they use strategies to approximate spellings of unfamiliar words during the drafting stage of the writing process.

10. How much time is required per week for effective spelling instruction?

Spelling programs typically recommend approximately 75 to 100 minutes of spelling instruction per week, but formal spelling instruction from books or lists is only the beginning of spelling instruction. As an integrated component of the language arts, spelling concepts should be highlighted in all areas of the curriculum. For example, spelling awareness can be most meaningfully fostered through editing and proofreading as part of the writing process. Furthermore, phonics, phonemic awareness, and word study provide important spelling knowledge. Spelling consciousness is best developed by integrating spelling instruction into all pertinent components of written language learning. It's difficult to know precisely how many minutes of instruction per week are required for effective spelling instruction, but 75 to 100 minutes per week that combines formal and informal spelling instruction is a good starting place (Chomsky, C., 1971, 1979; Henderson, 1989; Goodman, 1986).

Research in Action:

A Study of Spelling Errors in 18,599 Written
Compositions of Children in Grades 1–8

Ronald L. Cramer
James F. Cipielewski

Introduction

In the case of spelling, the cliché that we learn more from our failures than from our successes has a great deal of validity. Error analysis can be a fruitful approach to understanding how learning occurs and how improvements can be made in instructional procedures. It is therefore surprising that there have been relatively few substantial studies of children's spelling errors since Arthur Gates conducted the first important analysis of this kind in the mid-thirties. We believe that our recent research on the spelling errors of nearly 20,000 written compositions by children in grades 1–8 provides some additional answers to this important question: *What can we learn about children's spelling from studying their writing?*

> "It's a damn poor mind that can only think of one way to spell a word."
> ■
> Andrew Jackson

This article is organized around four major focal points: (1) purpose of the study, (2) data collection and analysis, (3) results and discussion, and (4) implications for instruction.

Purpose of the Study

The purpose of our study was to examine the spelling errors that arise in natural composition among children in grades 1–8. Our six specific purposes were to:

1. identify the most frequently misspelled words across grade levels
2. identify the most frequently misspelled words at each grade level
3. identify the linguistic error patterns represented in misspelled words
4. identify the linguistic and/or usage error patterns represented in misspelled words at each grade level
5. extend understanding of the developmental stages of spelling
6. derive information useful for developing an innovative spelling curriculum

Data Collection and Analysis
Data Collection

This study identified and categorized fifty-five types of spelling errors made by children in grades 1–8 in their unedited written compositions. The misspelled words were drawn from 18,599 compositions. Since subjects chose their own writing topics, the set of misspelled words represents a more natural sample than could be obtained under more constrained sampling procedures—for example, if subjects were given a writing prompt. As a result, the misspelled words and the error types identified in this study constitute an unusually valid sample of spelling errors.

We contacted principals in schools across the nation by mail in January of 1990, asking them to recommend teachers who might be willing to participate in a spelling error research project. A

total of 1,003 schools were initially contacted, and principals submitted 382 names of potential participants. As expected, due to the scope of the work required, some of those who had initially agreed to participate decided not to. Ultimately 256 teachers participated in the study, representing urban, suburban, and rural areas in all fifty states. The diversity of the participants in the study is evident in the schools' demographics. For example, participating schools included two schools in Hawaii with 52 percent and 65 percent Asian American enrollment respectively, a school in Los Angeles with 88 percent Hispanic American enrollment, a school in rural South Carolina with 61 percent African American enrollment, a small school in rural South Dakota with a total enrollment of 32 students, and a K–5 elementary school in Norcross, Georgia, with an enrollment of over 1,000 students. A complete list of the state, city, and teachers who participated in the study is included in Appendix A.

Participating teachers agreed to submit unedited compositions written by students on topics of their own choosing. Each teacher was asked to provide two sets of unedited and unprompted compositions in the spring, fall, and winter, from 1990 to 1991. A total of 18,599 unedited compositions was collected and analyzed. Table 1 shows the number of compositions submitted and analyzed by grade level across the collection time.

Table 1

Compositions Collected by Grade Level

	Spring 1990	Fall 1990	Winter 1991	Total
Grade 1	398	597	474	1,469
Grade 2	830	879	384	2,093
Grade 3	1,463	1,442	641	3,546
Grade 4	1,179	868	598	2,645
Grade 5	1,094	980	471	2,545
Grade 6	693	622	302	1,617
Grade 7	955	759	373	2,087
Grade 8	1,187	1,025	385	2,597
Total	7,799	7,172	3,628	18,599

Table 2 shows the number of compositions analyzed at each grade level and the average number of words per composition at each grade level. This information is used to arrive at the total number of words screened at each grade and the total number of words screened at all grades..

West Grade School, Stanfield, Oregon, Grade 5

Table 2

Number of Compositions Analyzed, Average Number of Words Per Composition, Total Number of Words Screened

	Number of Compositions Analyzed	Average Number of Words Per Composition	Total Number of Words Screened
Grade 1	1,469	35	51,415
Grade 2	2,093	50	104,650
Grade 3	3,546	69	244,674
Grade 4	2,645	80	211,600
Grade 5	2,545	90	229,050
Grade 6	1,617	97	156,849
Grade 7	2,087	123	256,701
Grade 8	2,597	127	329,819
Total/Avg.	18,599	83.9	1,584,758

Data Analysis

Analysis of data occurred over the course of two years, starting in the spring of 1990. As compositions were received, the process of recording spelling errors began. Readers were trained to identify and record spelling errors. Each reader completed the following tasks on each set of compositions read: (1) labeled compositions by state, grade level, and season submitted; (2) identified spelling errors and highlighted each error with a highlighting pen on the original composition; (3) listed each error on a separate recording sheet (on each individual composition, each error was counted only once in cases of repeated identical errors; if a word was spelled in several different ways, each of the novel spellings was counted); and (4) filed each set of compositions into a labeled folder when spelling-error identification had been completed.

After errors were recorded, the task of analyzing and categorizing them commenced. This analysis and categorization confirmed that the English language is not the chaotic beast of mythology it is often made out to be. On the contrary, it is systematic and reasonably predictable. As Henderson (1989) explains:

> Spelling knowledge has been shown to be much more than the ability to match letter to sound, albeit with many irregularities. Instead, spelling can now be described as a coherent and complex set of features that, when learned, vastly minimizes the difficulty of mastering the recognition and production of English words. The spelling of words must be remembered, of course, but it is the coherence of the spelling system that makes such remembering possible. (p. 3)

Why then is the myth of an irrational English spelling system so widely believed? Perhaps because many people suppose that spelling is governed by sound alone. But sound is not the sole governing principle of English spelling. It is true that the match between letters and sounds, particularly vowel sounds, is complex. Fortunately, there are other language features that govern the spelling system, thus facilitating its analysis and categorization. Four features that make English spelling reasonably predictable are

1. word structure and proximity principles
2. derivational principles associated with meaning
3. spelling patterns within words
4. regular consonant letter-sound matches

Cache la Poudre Junior High, La Porte, Colorado, Grade 7

In analyzing the misspellings in this survey, error categories were initially established based on the study of several hundred randomly selected compositions. Further exploratory analysis of errors soon demonstrated, however, that the initial set of error categories did not account for the range of errors showing up in the compositions. The research team eventually identified and defined fifty-five distinct error categories. Each error category was defined, described, and illustrated with examples. Table 3 shows the seven major kinds of misspellings this study defined and identified, as well as the number of subcategories within each major category.

Table 3
Seven Major Categories for Classifying Misspelled Words

Category of Error	Number of Error Subtypes
1. Vowel errors	22
2. Consonant errors	7
3. Word structure errors	5
4. Inflected ending errors	4
5. Compound word errors	4
6. Usage/convention errors	7
7. Twilight zone errors	6
Total	**55**

The category called "twilight zone errors" requires additional explanation. Some errors could not be easily categorized because the spellings were so truncated or bizarre that the target word could not be identified. Other errors such as omitting, adding, repeating, and scrambling letters are easy to classify but are distinct from linguistic, structural, or convention spelling errors. For example, omitting long *o* spelled *oa* is a different kind of spelling error than spelling the same vowel sound with the letters *oe*. At all grade levels, there were misspellings that could not be categorized as traditional vowel, consonant, structural, inflected, compound, or usage errors. As it turns out, adding, omitting, repeating, and scrambling letters are a major source of spelling errors. Table 4 shows examples of twilight zone errors.

Table 4
Twilight Zone Categories With Examples

Category	Example
Added letters	*drownded* for *drowned*
Omitted letters	*everthing* for *everything*
Repeated letters	*rememember* for *remember*
Scrambled/reversed	*feild* for *field*
Truncated/bizarre	*bcz* for *because*
Mispronounced	*wanna* for *want to*

Determining categories for classifying spelling errors presented significant difficulties for the research team. Much debate and many practical explorations preceded the final set of fifty-five categories described in Table 5. No claim is made, therefore, that the chosen categories exhaust every possibility for classifying errors. Nor is it claimed that this set of fifty-five categories is the only reasonable way to classify spelling errors. The categories do,

St. Richard's School, Indianapolis, Indiana, Grade 2

Table 5
Fifty-five Categories for Classifying Misspelled Words

Vowel Errors

1. Long *a*
2. Long *e*
3. Long *i*
4. Long *o*
5. /ü/
6. Short *a*
7. Short *e*
8. Short *i*
9. Short *o*
10. Short *u*
11. /ä/
12. /ô/
13. /ů/
14. /oi/
15. /ou/
16. /yü/
17. /ėr/
18. /ə/ (final syllable)
19. /ə/ (others)
20. Silent *e*, long vowel
21. Silent *e*, other
22. Silent *e*, overgeneralized

Consonant Errors

23. Consonant substitution
24. Single consonant, doubled
25. Double consonant in root
26. Consonant blend
27. Consonant digraph
28. Silent consonant
29. Complex consonant

Word Structure Errors: Affixes

30. Prefix
31. Suffix
32. *y* to *i* + suffix
33. Final *e* + suffix
34. Double consonant + suffix

Word Structure Errors: Inflected Endings

(-ed, -ing, -er, -est, -s, -es)
35. Inflected spelling
36. *y* to *i* + inflected ending
37. Final *e* + inflected ending
38. Double consonant with inflected ending

Table 5
Fifty-five Categories for Classifying Misspelled Words *(continued)*

Compound
39. Compound word spelling
40. Compound wrongly joined/hyphenated
41. Compound wrongly separated
42. Wrongly run together/separated

Usage Conventions
43. Capitalization
44. Abbreviation
45. Homophones
46. Easily confused pairs
47. Regularizing irregulars
48. Apostrophe with possessive
49. Apostrophe with contraction

Twilight Zone Errors
50. Added letters
51. Omitted letters
52. Repeated sequence
53. Scrambled letters
54. Truncated or bizarre
55. Mispronunciation

however, represent a defensible and reasonably exhaustive system of classification. All spelling errors identified in the study could be classified within the framework outlined in Table 5. To see examples of the types of errors indicated by each category, see Appendix B.

Since thousands of words were to be analyzed in the study, we assembled a team of error analyzers, consisting of graduate assistants, teachers, and editors. In addition, we prepared a guide called *Handbook for Misspelling Analyzers.* This forty-one-page handbook explained in detail the error classification system and provided appropriate examples. We also provided the spelling analyzers extensive training in small-group sessions to assure that everyone approached the classification process with the same understanding. In instances where an analyzer had difficulty classifying a word, the question was submitted to one of the authors of this article (R. Cramer) for final determination. Although extreme care was taken, undoubtedly mistakes were made. Nevertheless, the system worked well and with relatively few instances of difficulty in classifying spelling errors according to the error types established for this study.

Table 6 is a sample of how spelling errors were classified. Keep in mind that a given misspelling can exhibit more than one spelling error. The error-type numbers correspond with the error categories in Table 5.

Table 6
Spelling Error Analysis

Target Word	Misspelling	Error Type, 1 to 55
1. a lot	alot	42
2. assignment	assingment	28, 53
3. believe	belive	2
4. couldn't	couldt	49
5. died	dide	35, 53
6. especially	expeshly	23, 27, 51, 34
7. excuse	exuce	51, 29
8. nervous	nearvise	17, 31, 18, 22
9. New Year's	newyears	43, 40, 48
10. practice	practes	8, 29

To examine how the system worked, look at the misspelling of *especially*. Error category 23 indicates the substitution of the consonant *x* for the consonant *s*; error category 27 indicates the misspelling of the digraph *ci* as *sh*; error category 51 indicates the missing *a*; error category 34 indicates the dropping of an *l* with the addition of the suffix.

Results and Discussion

This study considered two major types of spelling errors: (1) the most frequently misspelled words across and within grade levels and (2) the fifty-five specific sources of spelling errors within words. In this section, we present and discuss various lists of frequently misspelled words and data concerning sources of errors within words.

Frequently Misspelled Words

There are any number of categories of frequently misspelled words that one could determine from the data collected for this study. However, this article will limit itself to a discussion of three lists of frequently misspelled words: 100 Most Frequently Misspelled Words Across Eight Grade Levels, 25 Most Frequently Misspelled Words at Each Grade Level, and The Most Frequently Misspelled Homophones.

100 Most Frequently Misspelled Words Across Eight Grade Levels Table 7 (p. 24) shows the hundred most commonly misspelled words across grade levels. The words that appear on this list are virtually unavoidable in almost any type of writing: poetry, narrative, or expository. Since the list contains words of the highest frequency in reading, writing, and speaking, it is easy to see why mastery of this list alone would vastly improve the spelling power of the poorest spellers, as well as upgrade the spelling competence of more advanced spellers.

It should be noted that the hundred most frequently misspelled words are not identical to the hundred most frequently used words. When Carroll, Davies, and Richman (1971) analyzed the frequency with which words appear in English, they found that the 1,000 most frequently used words accounted for almost 90 percent of written text. Because these words are used so frequently, one might think they might also account for many spelling errors. A comparison of these two top 100 lists, using regression analysis, finds that there is not a strong link between them. The frequency of the words accounts for only 4 percent of the variance in the hundred most frequently misspelled words. (See Figure 1.)

It is likely that spelling instruction could be significantly improved if one knew in advance what problems children are most likely to encounter. An examination of this list, along with

Figure 1: Regression Analysis of the Most Frequent 100 Words in Appearance vs. Misspelling

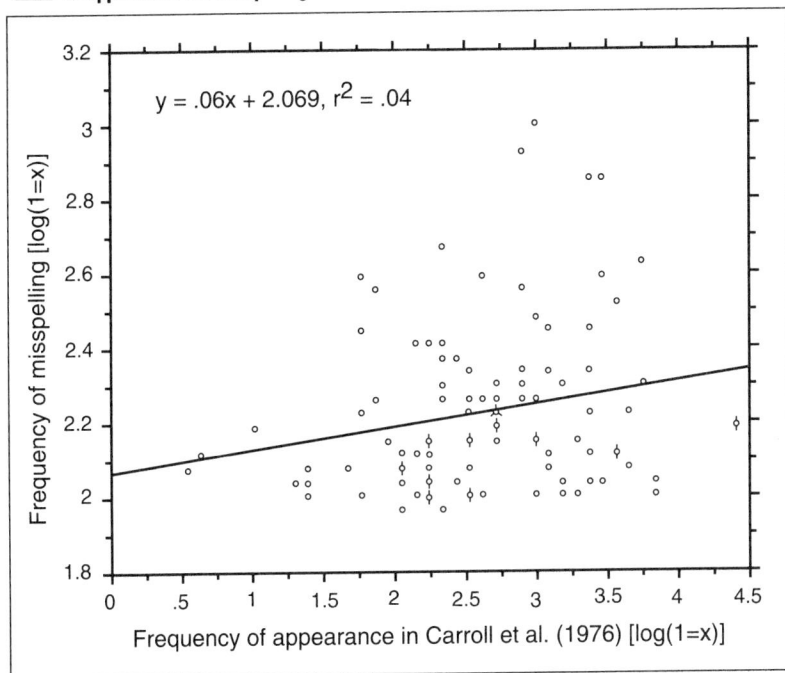

$$y = .06x + 2.069, r^2 = .04$$

Y-axis: Frequency of misspelling [log(1=x)]

X-axis: Frequency of appearance in Carroll et al. (1976) [log(1=x)]

(Frequencies were converted to logarithms because of the highly skewed nature of word frequencies.)

an awareness of the types of spelling errors certain word features tend to generate, makes some predictions quite feasible. For example, some of the more predictable errors involve homophones, words with an apostrophe, words starting with *a* or *be* that are often wrongly joined or separated, and compound words. There are other predictable spelling problems presented on this list, though they constitute a smaller percentage of potential error generating properties than the four mentioned above.

Table 7

100 Most Frequently Misspelled Words Across Eight Grade Levels

1. too	35. probably	69. doesn't
2. a lot	36. don't	70. usually
3. because	37. sometimes	71. clothes
4. there	38. off	72. scared
5. their	39. everybody	73. everyone
6. that's	40. heard	74. have
7. they	41. always	75. swimming
8. it's	42. I	76. about
9. when	43. something	77. first
10. favorite	44. would	78. happened
11. went	45. want	79. Mom
12. Christmas	45. and	80. especially
13. were	47. Halloween	81. school
14. our	48. house	82. getting
15. they're	49. once	83. started
16. said	50. to	84. was
17. know	51. like	85. which
18. you're	52. whole	86. stopped
19. friend	53. another	87. two
20. friends	54. believe	88. Dad
21. really	55. I'm	89. took
22. finally	56. thought	90. friend's
23. where	57. let's	91. presents
24. again	58. before	92. are
25. then	59. beautiful	93. morning
26. didn't	60. everything	94. could
27. people	61. very	95. around
28. until	62. into	96. buy
29. with	63. caught	97. maybe
30. different	64. one	98. family
31. outside	65. Easter	99. pretty
32. we're	66. what	100. tried
33. through	67. there's	
34. upon	68. little	

The most pervasive problem is the spelling of homophones, which constitute about 20 percent of the 100 Most Frequently Misspelled Words Across Eight Grade Levels shown in Table 7. The major problem children have with homophones is using them correctly; spelling them correctly is also a problem, but of lesser dimension.

A second problem concerns words that contain an apostrophe, which make up about 10 percent of the 100 Most Frequently Misspelled Words, some of which are also homophones. Joining words with an apostrophe is important knowledge for spellers to acquire, since the words that are most often used as contractions are among the high frequency words in written English.

A third highly predictable spelling problem represented in the 100 Most Frequently Misspelled Words involves words that lend themselves to inappropriate separation or joining. Some words such as *a little* spelled *alittle* were improperly joined. The ubiquitous misspelling of *a lot* as *alot* clearly outdistances all other problems of this type, but many children have a related problem that shows up in words of this sort: *because* spelled *be cause, around* spelled *a round, believe* spelled *be lieve, another* spelled *a nother, again* spelled *a gain, always* spelled *al ways* or *all ways.* Clearly writers had difficulty determining whether or not similarly sounding words or groups of words should be joined or separated.

A fourth highly predictable spelling problem illustrated in this list is the misspelling of compounds by wrongly separating them or, less commonly, by wrongly joining an open compound or joining a compound with a hyphen: *outside* spelled *out side, ice cream* spelled *icecream, baby-sit* spelled *babysit,* and so on.

Most Frequently Misspelled Words at Each Grade Level Table 8 lists the twenty-five most frequently misspelled words at each grade level. Close examination reveals a startling amount of overlap across grade levels from one through eight. Certain words are among the twenty-five most frequently misspelled on all eight lists: *too, their, there, because.* Many other words appear on four, five, six, or seven of the lists. Moreover, when this list is extended

Table 8

25* Most Frequently Misspelled Words at Each Grade Level

Grade 1

because	too	with	was	were
when	said	have	would	people
like	there	very	are	about
they	house	friend	want	Christmas
went	know	my	friends	play

Grade 2

because	went	friends	would	Easter
too	their	were	upon	once
they	Christmas	said	know	again
when	people	our	friend	didn't
there	favorite	a lot	outside	scared

Grade 3

too	Christmas	favorite	upon	then
because	were	when	with	I
there	said	friend	our	always
their	went	know	really	finally
a lot	they	that's	friends	again

Grade 4

too	favorite	they're	again	outside
a lot	that's	were	they	said
because	our	it's	Christmas	we're
there	when	know	went	different
their	really	finally	until	sometimes

*See Appendix C for the 100 Most Frequently Misspelled Words at Each Grade.

Table 8
25* Most Frequently Misspelled Words at Each Grade Level *(continued)*

Grade 5

a lot	favorite	it's	until	through
too	that's	really	friend	were
their	finally	different	they	believe
there	our	where	you're	know
because	they're	again	friends	something

Grade 6

a lot	their	everything	until	college
too	there	finally	different	they
it's	you're	our	really	through
because	favorite	probably	usually	where
that's	were	they're	beautiful	we're

Grade 7

there	it's	Easter	Christmas	until
a lot	because	they	off	buy
too	don't	you're	where	let's
their	probably	finally	Halloween	really
that's	they're	our	didn't	then

Grade 8

a lot	that's	don't	can't	didn't
too	there	we're	usually	off
it's	they're	finally	doesn't	TV
you're	because	there's	really	until
their	probably	where	allowed	something

*See Appendix C for the 100 Most Frequently Misspelled Words at Each Grade.

to the 100 Most Frequently Misspelled Words at Each Grade Level, the amount of overlap is quite startling. Table 9 illustrates the extent of the overlap in misspellings between grade levels. Clearly if one could reduce the errors children make on a relatively small subset of troublesome words, substantial progress in spelling proficiency would be made.

It is manifest from this study that the words primary grade children misspell are, in many instances, the words intermediate and junior high school children continue to misspell. At the same time, an examination of the spelling curriculum taught in many schools throughout the nation will show that many of these often misspelled words are indeed taught fairly early in the spelling curriculum. Unfortunately, it is also true that many of these words are taught only once within the span of an eight-year spelling curriculum, the norm in most schools throughout the country. How did this state of affairs come about? What can be done to improve this situation? These issues will be discussed later in this article.

Table 9
Correlation Between Frequencies of Misspellings by Grade Level

	Grade 1	Grade 2	Grade 3	Grade 4	Grade 5	Grade 6	Grade 7
Grade 2	0.83						
Grade 3	0.74	0.91					
Grade 4	0.63	0.83	0.90				
Grade 5	0.53	0.75	0.85	0.91			
Grade 6	0.40	0.60	0.70	0.80	0.85		
Grade 7	0.44	0.66	0.77	0.83	0.87	0.83	
Grade 8	0.33	0.53	0.64	0.75	0.83	0.91	0.86

All values of r are significant at the .01 level of significance.

Homophones

Homophones are a significant spelling problem. Difficulty spelling homophones begins early and increases across grade levels. For example, homophones constitute 2.4 percent of the spelling errors committed at grade 1 and grow steadily through higher grades, culminating at 8 percent of the errors at grade 8.

There are three likely explanations for the high incidence of homophone errors. First, children's reading and writing vocabularies grow substantially from grade 1 through grade 8. Consequently, with more homophones available for writing, the possibility for errors increases with age. Second, as children mature, they write longer compositions; consequently they use and misspell the common homophones more frequently. Third, progress in correctly spelling the most frequently used homophones is slow. For example, distinguishing between *too* and *to* and *their* and *there* continues to plague students across all grade levels included in this study. When homophones are misspelled, it is more often a failure of correct usage and meaning than difficulty with the orthography, especially in the case of common homophones. The writer's problem is linking the correct orthography to the intended usage. Such errors may also, in part, be attributed to "slips," or the inadvertent writing of the wrong homophone as the student's mind is on the process of composing (Wing and Baddeley, 1980). This may be compounded by a relative infrequency of encountering all the forms during reading. Students who read less, therefore, seem to be more likely to commit errors when spelling the less frequent analogs of homophones. Table 10 shows the twenty most frequently misspelled homophones across grade levels 1–8.

Table 10
Most Frequently Misspelled Homophones Across Grades Levels 1–8

too	they're	would	there's
there	know	to	clothes
their	you're	whole	two
it's	through	let's	presents
our	heard	one	buy

Sources of Errors Within Words

When analyzing spelling errors, it is important to differentiate between errors caused by misunderstanding how to spell words correctly and errors caused by inattention, often called "slips" (Wing and Baddeley, 1980). There is evidence that among the spelling errors collected for this study there are a sizable number of the latter type—words that are known but misspelled because of inattention. One indication is the fact that several types of errors show little decline over time, especially scrambled letters and omitted letters. These appear in the top ten types of errors at every grade level. The most obvious remedies for these types of errors are more attention during the writing and, perhaps more importantly, giving students ample time and effective strategies for copyediting their writing.

Table 11 shows the order, from most frequent to least frequent, of the fifty-five error types for combined grade levels 1–8. Across all grade levels, omitted letters proved to be the single greatest cause of spelling errors, with homophones a close second. Table 11 suggests an interesting piece of information not generally reported in the literature on spelling errors of children. Omitted letters (number 1), scrambled letters (number 4), and added letters (number 12) are major factors in generating spelling errors. These three error categories are seldom taken into account in spelling instruction or in the preparation of instructional materials for teaching spelling. Table 11 also reveals that running together words that should be separated (number 10), *alot* for *a lot,* and separating words that are one word, *a nother* for *another,* also ranks among the top ten error-generating types. Not surprisingly, problems associated with vowels and consonants round out the top ten error types.

Table 11
Top Error Categories for Combined Grade Levels 1–8

1. Omitted letters
2. Homophones
3. Consonant substitution
4. Scrambled letters
5. Schwa (other)
6. Short *e*
7. Long *e*
8. Schwa final syllable
9. Consonant blend
10. Run together/separated
11. Consonant digraph
12. Added letters
13. Short *i*
14. Double consonant in root
15. Inflected spelling
16. Compound wrongly separated
17. Apostrophe with contraction
18. Complex consonant
19. Vowel: /ô/
20. Capitalization
21. Long *a*
22. Silent *e* overgeneralized
23. Single consonant doubled
24. Silent *e* other
25. Short *u*
26. Apostrophe with possessive
27. Long *i*
28. Silent *e* long vowel
29. Double consonant + inflected ending
30. Compound word spelling
31. Vowel: /ėr/
32. Long *o*
33. Easily confused pairs
34. Vowel: /ü/
35. Suffix spelling
36. Truncated/bizarre
37. Silent consonant
38. Mispronunciation
39. Compound wrongly joined
40. Final *e* + inflected ending
41. Double consonant + suffix
42. Vowel: /ou/
43. *y* to *i* + inflected ending
44. Short *o*
45. Short *a*
46. Vowel: /ü/
47. Final *e* + suffix
48. Regularizing irregulars
49. Vowel: /ä/
50. Vowel: /yü/
51. Repeated sequence
52. Prefix spelling
53. Abbreviation
54. Vowel: /oi/
55. *y* to *i* + suffix

For information about the error types when considered across three levels—Primary 1–3, Intermediate 4–6, and Upper 7–8—see Appendix D.

Table 12 classifies spelling errors across seven major error types: vowel, consonant, structural, inflected, compound, usage, and twilight zone. When spelling errors are ranked by major error type, the following findings are supported:

1. Vowel errors are the number one error type across all grade levels, 1–8.
2. Consonant errors are the second most common error type across grades 1–5. For grades 6–8, however, consonant errors rank third or fourth.
3. Twilight zone errors are the third most common error type for all grade levels except grade 7, where they rank fourth.
4. Usage errors are the fourth most common error type for grades 1–5. For grades 6–8, usage errors are the second most common error type.
5. Compound word errors are the fifth most common error type for all grades except grade 1, where they rank seventh.
6. Structure errors are the sixth most common error type for grades 1 and 6–8. For grades 2–5, structure errors rank seventh.
7. Inflected word errors are the seventh most common error type for grades 6–8, the sixth for grades 2–5, and the fifth for grade 1.

There are few, if any, surprises in the findings outlined above. It is to be expected that vowel and consonant errors would rank first and second as sources of spelling errors. Vowel spellings are highly variable, as Hanna, Hodges, and Hanna (1982) have shown, and, like consonants, they are potential sources of error in all words. The research on developmental spelling supports this finding as well (Beers and Henderson, 1977).

Consonants are less variable than vowels, but they make up the largest proportion of potential error generating features of words. This finding is also expected. The fact that consonant errors decline over time suggests that students are able to recognize and use the phonologically regular nature of consonants to spell more accurately. Perhaps the least expected finding is that twilight zone errors rank third. The relatively high ranking of this error type is influenced by errors due to omitted, scrambled, and added letter(s). Usage errors rank fourth. This ranking is undoubtedly influenced by homophone errors, which rank high as an error source at primary, intermediate, and upper grade levels. Compound errors, somewhat surprisingly, rank fifth ahead of structure and inflected error types. It is likely, however, that the frequent misspelling of a single word, *alot* for *a lot,* which was assigned to the compound error category, may have influenced this outcome. Structure and inflected errors ranked sixth and seventh, respectively. Since both of these categories deal with structural spelling errors, their close ranking suggests internal consistency in the data reported in this study.

Table 12
Rank of Major Error Types by Grade Level

Error Name	Grade							
	1	2	3	4	5	6	7	8
Vowel	1	1	1	1	1	1	1	1
Consonant	2	2	2	2	2	4	3	4
Structure	6	7	7	7	7	6	6	6
Inflected	5	6	6	6	6	7	7	7
Compound	7	5	5	5	5	5	5	5
Usage	4	4	4	4	4	2	2	2
Twilight Zone	3	3	3	3	3	3	4	3

Table 13 reports the proportion of major error types by grade level across seven major error types: vowel, consonant, structure, inflected, compound, usage, and twilight zone. When spelling errors are considered in terms of proportion of errors that may be attributed to error types, the following findings are supported.

1. There is a substantial and consistent decline in vowel errors across grade levels. Nearly half of the spelling errors made by first graders, 49 percent, involve vowel errors. By eighth grade, vowel errors have declined substantially, to 29 percent.

2. There is a small but consistent decline in consonant spelling errors across grade levels, ranging from 18 percent of the errors at grade 1 to 15 percent at grade 8.

3. The proportion of structure errors increases steadily but moderately across grade levels, ranging from about 4 percent at grade 1 to nearly 6 percent at grade 8.

4. The proportion of inflected spelling errors remains quite steady across grade levels, with only moderate fluctuation from one grade level to the next. Inflected errors account for about 5 percent of first and eighth grade spelling errors.

5. The proportion of compound spelling errors increases steadily from 3 percent in first grade to 11 percent in eighth grade.

6. The proportion of usage errors increases steadily from 6 percent in first grade to 19 percent in eighth grade.
7. The proportion of twilight zone errors remains remarkably consistent across grade levels, with only moderate fluctuation from one grade level to the next. Twilight zone errors account for about 15 percent of first and eighth grade spelling errors.

Table 13
Proportion of Major Error Types by Grade Level

Error Name	Grade							
	1	2	3	4	5	6	7	8
Vowel	.488	.438	.402	.361	.434	.307	.318	.290
Consonant	.177	.183	.185	.168	.165	.149	.156	.148
Structure	.041	.044	.043	.051	.049	.056	.056	.056
Inflected	.051	.053	.057	.058	.060	.056	.053	.054
Compound	.034	.056	.060	.081	.083	.110	.096	.110
Usage	.058	.091	.104	.122	.140	.165	.176	.188
Twilight Zone	.151	.137	.148	.159	.161	.158	.146	.154

The substantial improvement in vowel spelling across grade levels and the moderate improvement in consonant spelling is an important finding, though not unexpected. Structural and inflected errors, however, do not show improvement over time. On the contrary, the proportion of such errors increases from first to eighth grade. The moderate increases in such errors may be due, in part, to the higher proportion of such words in the writing vocabularies of older students compared to younger students.

Both compound and usage errors increase substantially over time. The increase in the proportion of usage errors may be influenced by the increasing prevalence of homophone misspelling as students proceed up the grades. It is not as obvious why the proportion of compound spelling errors increases over time. It is possible that more of the kinds of words included in this category are available in older students' vocabularies, although this is not as obvious in the case of compounds as it is for structural words and homophones. The relative increase in these errors may reflect children's increasingly sophisticated oral language, which often does not have commensurate orthographic knowledge to support it in print. Other oral language constructs that cause confusion in print are contractions. Although it is easy to use contracted forms in speech, children find it relatively difficult to determine where to place apostrophes or to distinguish the contracted form from a regularly spelled homophonic form in writing. *Your* and *you're* and *there* and *they're* are good examples of this confusion.

Implications for Instruction

Most people value the ability to spell correctly very highly. Have you notised how quickly people judge educational qualifications and even intelligence on the basis of a few inocent spelling errors? Suppose, for example, the authors of this article didn't know they had misspelled *noticed* and *innocent* in the previous sentence. Many people would make adverse judgments about the authors' educational qualifications on the basis of these two spelling errors. Did you make such a snap judgment a few sentences back? As we consider the implications of this study, keep in mind that society considers spelling important. Rightly or wrongly, society uses spelling as a barometer of capabilities it is not well suited to measure. Perhaps you do too. We want to conclude this article by explaining how the data presented supports two related ideas: (1) certain aspects of the spelling curriculum need to be rethought, and (2) schools need to put greater emphasis on spelling instruction.

Rethinking the Spelling Curriculum

This study has shown the importance of selecting the appropriate words for instruction, recycling, and reviewing; choosing the right linguistic and related patterns for organizing and sequencing instruction; and developing a research-based rationale for constructing word lists. We have seen that the common words children use in daily writing are frequently misspelled. Many of the words children in the primary grades misspell continue to be misspelled by children in intermediate grades, and many of the words children in intermediate grades misspell continue to be misspelled by children in upper grades. Teachers would not be surprised, for instance, to know that the word *because* ranks among the ten most frequently misspelled words at every grade level, 1–8. Other common words have a similar history. If this study had included high school and college subjects, it might have discovered similar problems at these levels as well. Anecdotal evidence from teachers and professors suggests that this is highly likely.

However, it is not just the hundred most frequently misspelled words that must be learned. An educated person ought to command a basic spelling vocabulary of perhaps 10,000 words. And as many as 6,000 words ought to be included in the spelling curriculum of grades 1–8. Furthermore, it is not sufficient to simply teach words. There are basic spelling strategies and principles of spelling instruction that must be absorbed along with the learning of a spelling vocabulary. For example, every intermediate and upper grade student ought to understand and use the following spelling-meaning principle: *Words related in meaning are often related in spelling even though changes occur in the sounds within a given word.* But systematic instruction related to this principle cannot occur when spelling lists are based on haphazard criteria.

New Lexington Elementary School, El Monte, California, Grade 3

Lists based solely on frequency, content, or literature will not expose students to systematic spelling-meaning connections. The criteria for spelling lists must include frequency in written language, frequency of misspelling, developmental spelling stages, and linguistic, structural, sound, and proximity principles. Yes, content words dealing with literature, social studies, science, health, math, and English should be taught, but they cannot be the sole organizing principle.

This study has shown that homophones are an especially difficult spelling problem. The difficulty begins at first grade with words such as *too, their,* and *there* and continues to claim an increasingly larger proportion of spelling errors as children proceed up the grades. There may be reasonable explanations about why the problem gets worse as schooling continues, but the reasons don't remedy the problem. Those who prepare materials for spelling instruction must address the homophone problem as both a meaning and a spelling issue.

In the past, spelling instruction has proceeded on the assumption that one exposure to a basic word is sufficient. The results of this study demonstrate that this assumption is incorrect. Many children in grades 1–8 do not learn the basic words with one exposure. Indeed it may take some children two to eight years or more to learn certain basic words. Furthermore, spelling instruc-

Rice Elementary School, San Carlos, Arizona, Grade 4

tion has proceeded on a thin base of spelling research. We have, in the past, known little about the relative importance of specific error types. Although this study has begun to fill in some of this missing data, additional research is needed to more adequately answer questions about how children learn to spell, what words should be taught, and what strategies work best. As we develop answers to these questions, we will be better able to construct innovative instructional materials that work for a larger proportion of children who need all the help they can get in learning to spell.

Improving Spelling Instruction in Schools

Words are vehicles for our written ideas. A good idea poorly presented, whether due to inaccurate spelling or inadequate writing, will not get the attention it deserves. Unfortunately, in the past decade, many schools have abandoned formal spelling instruction, replacing it in some venues with lists of words based on dubious premises. Some schools have adopted so-called high frequency lists, some are using content-based lists, and still others are using literature-based lists. What these schools have in common is inadequate criteria for preparing word lists and little or nothing to guide teachers as they try to implement the lists in classrooms. More often than not, little thought has been given to these important questions:

1. What words should be taught?
2. How should words be chosen, organized, and presented?
3. How should words be organized across grade levels?
4. What word study and writing activities ought to accompany spelling instruction?
5. What words should be recycled and reviewed, how often, and by what criteria?
6. What relationship does spelling have with reading and writing?
7. Do the words taught suit the children's stages of spelling development?

Spelling instruction is too important to become the victim of the latest educational fad. There is certainly room for various approaches to teaching spelling. However, if we fail to subject spelling instruction to a rigorous examination of sound premises, careful research, and examined practices, there will be more and more students leaving our schools unable to spell such basic words as *because, a lot*, and *too*.

Ronald L. Cramer *is a Professor of Education and Chairman of the Department of Reading and Language Arts at Oakland University in Rochester, Michigan.*

James Cipielewski *is an Assistant Professor of Reading and Language Arts at Oakland University in Rochester, Michigan.*

Using the Research:

Developing a Spelling Curriculum

Kathryn Marine

Introduction

The movement towards integrating the language arts has dramatically changed the way many educators teach reading and writing, probably for the better. However, some teachers are having difficulty determining where spelling fits into the new curriculum design. Many teachers are still required to give a spelling grade on student report cards. And many parents consider spelling to be a very important skill. In today's changing curriculum, spelling is one area of student competence that parents still are able to evaluate, and, rightly or wrongly, they may judge a school's program based on their children's spelling proficiency. There is no argument that correct spelling is an essential part of effective written communication, and it is certainly an important outcome of most curricula. But how does spelling fit into an integrated language arts curriculum?

Spelling is not something that students learn magically. While spelling should be emphasized in the context of students' writing, it is also important that students receive explicit instruction about spelling concepts and generalizations (Gentry and Gillet, 1993; Buchanan, 1989; Henderson, 1989). In addition to mastering a set of words, students need to recognize when they have misspelled a word. Think of the ability to recognize misspellings as *developing spelling consciousness.*

R. L. Cramer's Research in Action project (1995), done in conjunction with ScottForesman, provided extensive information about what students do when they misspell words. This study showed how creative children can be when they are trying to spell a difficult word. For example, students participating in Research in Action misspelled the word *because* 820 times, coming up with 175 unique misspellings. Table 1 shows the most common misspellings of *because.*

Table 1
Five Most Common Misspellings of *because*

becuse
cause
becase
becaus
becouse

Notice that there is really nothing too unusual in any of these misspellings. Children are misspelling the difficult parts of the word. The most bizarre misspelling of *because* was *lz*, but when you consider that it was written by a first grader early in the school year, it really isn't all that bizarre.

The findings of Research in Action showed that students can be very literal when they are misspelling words. Perhaps the sixth grader who wrote *loss Vegas* when telling about a family vacation was describing the outcome of the vacation, as well as the destination. And who knows how much the second grader who wrote *noosepaper* knows about newspapers, but some might say her description was fairly accurate.

The Research in Action project also revealed important information about what spelling concepts should be taught and when they should be taught. Using this information can yield a very effective spelling curriculum. Specifically, this article will examine what Research in Action told us about the spelling concepts that should be taught; the most appropriate focus of spelling instruction at the primary, intermediate, and upper elementary grades; and some sources for finding appropriate words.

What Concepts Should Be Taught in a Spelling Curriculum?

The Research in Action project analyzed spelling errors based on sound, structure, meaning, and the seemingly unexplainable, or Twilight Zone. Not surprisingly, we found differences in the types of spelling errors made by students based on their developmental level. Table 2 shows that at the primary grades four of the five most common types of errors involve misspelling vowel and consonant sounds. In the intermediate grades, the most common student spelling errors have moved away from sound patterns, and by the upper elementary grades, the most common type of error is meaning related. Notice, however, that the category Omitted Letters appears in the top five at all three levels and the category Scrambled Letters appears in the upper two levels. Although these spelling issues have never been addressed directly in traditional spelling instruction, we can't ignore that leaving letters out of words and getting them mixed up within words are important issues to face in helping students develop spelling consciousness. (For a complete list of error category information from Research in Action, see Appendix D.)

Table 2

Top Five Categories of Errors from Research in Action

Primary Grades 1–3	Intermediate Grades 4–6	Upper Grades 7–8
1. Consonant substitution	Omitted letters	Homophones
2. Omitted letters	Homophones	Omitted letters
3. Short *e*	Consonant substitution	Schwa
4. Consonant blends	Scrambled letters	Scrambled letters
5. Long *e*	Schwa	Consonant substitution

From the information gathered in Research in Action, we believe there are six basic elements that should be part of a spelling curriculum.

1. *Spelling Patterns.* These should start with patterns that can be generalized to a large number of commonly used words, including common spellings of vowel sounds and consonant sounds. Some examples of spelling patterns include the sound /ē/ in *feed* and *beak* and the sound /f/ in *farm* and *phone*. We know there is a need for teaching spelling patterns when students make spelling errors such as *blede* for *bleed* or *truk* for *truck*.

2. *Spelling Structure Rules.* Specifically, these are the rules that can be applied to a large number of words. They include the rules for forming plurals such as whether to add *-s* or *-es*, the rules for adding *-ed* and *-ing* such as when consonants are doubled, and rules for adding prefixes and suffixes. A need for teaching spelling structure rules is evident when we see spelling errors such as *tride* for *tried*, *foxs* for *foxes*, or *finaly* for *finally*.

3. *Spelling and Meaning Relationships.* These are relationships in which the meaning of a word affects its spelling. Students com-

monly have difficulty with homophones, easily confused words such as *except* and *accept,* contractions, and related words such as *sign* and *signal.* Meaning-based instruction would also help prevent errors such as *helth* for *health* and *narritive* for *narrative.* If students know that *heal* and *health* and *narrate* and *narrative* are related in spelling and meaning, they probably won't make these kinds of errors.

4. *Developing Spelling Consciousness.* This addresses what children do when they misspell words and helps them focus on patrolling their own spelling. Developing spelling consciousness helps students understand why, for example, they misspell *hungry* as *hungery, surprise* as *suprise,* and *said* as *siad.*

5. *Spelling Strategies.* These are strategies that students can use to learn to spell words that cause problems for them. For example, the strategy of pronouncing for spelling asks students to concentrate on saying a word such as *hamster* correctly so they don't misspell it by writing *hampster* or saying a word like *especially* correctly so they don't write it *expecially.*

6. *Most Commonly Misspelled Words.* Because there is a group of words students are most likely to use and misspell, it makes sense that they be part of a spelling curriculum. (You'll find the hundred most commonly misspelled words at each grade level in Appendix C.)

What Concepts Should Be Taught at Your Grade Level?

By analyzing the information from the Research in Action project, we have been able to get a very clear picture of how the types of spelling errors that students make change as they develop as spellers. Such changes directly affect the focus of spelling instruction at each grade level. For example, first graders make very few spelling errors with homophones, but by sixth grade, homophones are the single most common source of spelling errors. On the other hand, sixth graders make very few spelling errors with short vowel sounds, but short vowels are commonly misspelled by first graders.

The information from Research in Action has helped us develop appropriate curriculum content for each grade. The Suggested Spelling Curriculum Charts in Appendix E show the progression of concepts and skills that might make up a very effective spelling curriculum for primary, intermediate, and upper elementary grades. Following are some of the significant changes that occur as students develop as spellers in grades one through eight.

Sound Patterns

In first grade, when children are just beginning to use written language, it is important to emphasize the most simple and common spelling patterns such as the sound /a/ spelled *a* in *can* and *hat* or the sound /k/ spelled *ck* in *pack* and *bucket*. However, as children develop as spellers, they need to be exposed to more varied and difficult spelling patterns. For example, the sound /j/ can be spelled many different ways: *jump, gentle, large, badger, edge, adjust, soldier*. The more information children have about the ways English sounds can be spelled, the better equipped they are to develop their own spelling consciousness. As children learn more about English spelling, they become better at figuring out how to spell new words, or, at the very least, they learn how to look up words they don't know in the dictionary. However, by the upper elementary grades we recommend a minimal emphasis on sound patterns, concentrating on more unusual patterns such as the sound /s/ spelled *ps* at the beginning of *psychology* or the sound /z/ spelled *sp* in the middle of *raspberry*.

Spelling Structure Rules

Early on, students need to learn the rudimentary principles of forming plurals and adding endings. As students develop as spellers and learners, they need to learn the rules that govern these principles. Although students should have learned the basic rules that govern spelling structure by third grade, it is not uncommon for sixth-, seventh-, and eighth-grade teachers to see spelling mistakes like these: *crys* for *cries* or *planed* for *planned*. Although structure rules should not be emphasized at the upper elementary grades, they still need to be taught and reviewed. And at the middle and upper grades, students need to learn about irregular spelling structure issues such as adding -s or -es to words that end in o or adding k when adding -ed or -ing to a word that ends in c—panicked. (See Appendix E for a more complete list of structure patterns.)

Spelling and Meaning

As students acquire larger vocabularies, the emphasis of spelling instruction should shift from sound patterns and structure to meaning (Beers, 1980; Buchanan, 1989). First grade is probably too early to emphasize spelling and meaning. However, by second grade, we see students making spelling errors related to a word's meaning, especially errors with homophones. Homophones should be taught early and often. Most homophone errors are caused by just a few common culprits. The homophone groups in Table 3 account for over half of all the spelling errors students in Research in Action made with homophones. As a matter of fact, *too* was the single most commonly misspelled word across grades 1–8 in Research in Action.

Table 3
Most Commonly Misspelled Homophones

to	there	its	your
too	their	it's	you're
two	they're		

Contractions also cause their own unique spelling problems. As any teacher knows, once students learn how to use apostrophes, they start to use them everywhere—except where they're supposed to. Contractions and homophones are among the most commonly misspelled words. (Lists of the most commonly misspelled words at each grade level are included in Appendix C.)

Spelling Consciousness

Traditionally spelling instruction has concentrated on sound, structure, and meaning; however, the Research in Action project helped us see that we need to broaden the scope of spelling instruction. Developing spelling consciousness, or tuning students in to their own strengths and needs as spellers, is an idea that sprang directly from Research in Action. In first grade, this means helping students realize that many words they read and write frequently, such as *one, said,* or *again,* don't fit into the regular English spelling patterns that they've been learning. By second grade, however, some patterns of spelling errors begin occurring that can't be easily remedied by teaching more spelling sound patterns or rules. Although we classified these errors as Twilight Zone in the research, they actually were explainable. The spelling errors in Table 4 were made by students in Research in Action and classified in Twilight Zone categories.

Table 4
Sample Errors in Twilight Zone Categories

Omitted Letters	Added Letters	Scrambled Letters
cabnet	athalete	dosen't
favrite	didin't	feild

The errors in Table 4 aren't bizarre misspellings. As a matter of fact, they are very logical. They're mostly the kinds of spelling errors that occur when we ask students to sound out words. Developing spelling consciousness is aimed at getting students to focus on what they personally are doing when they misspell. For example, a student who misspells *didn't* by writing *didin't* is probably adding a sound when pronouncing the word. This self-awareness becomes increasingly important as students grow as spellers. Another misspelling made by a student in Research in Action was *qwiditsidents.* This first grader's attempt to spell *coincidence* may appear rather wild at first glance, but closer examination reveals that this young person actually knew a lot about the sound patterns of the English language.

Table 5
Spelling Strategies

Strategies	How to Use Them
Steps for Spelling New Words	1. Look at the word and say it. 2. Spell it aloud. 3. Think about it. 4. Picture it. 5. Look at it and write it. 6. Cover, write, and check it.
Rhyming Helpers	Link a word with a rhyming word that is spelled the same at the end: un<u>less</u>—m<u>ess</u>
Problem Parts	Identify the part of the word that gives you problems and study it extra hard: <u>wr</u>ong lau<u>gh</u>ed
Creating Memory Tricks	Link tricky words with a memory helper that has the same problem letters: Tell that mos<u>qui</u>to to <u>qui</u>t biting me.
Using Meaning Helpers	Pair a word with a shorter, related word that gives a sound clue: act—action heal—health
Divide and Conquer	Divide a word into smaller parts: team/mate beauti/ful ar/ti/fi/cial
Pronouncing for Spelling	Pronounce a word correctly: pro•<u>ba</u>•bly Or make up a secret pronunciation: choc•<u>o</u>•late

Spelling Strategies

Once students begin to identify words that give them problems, they need ways to deal with those words. That's where spelling strategies come in. The strategies in Table 5 are practical, workable ways to help children remember words that are difficult for them. The strategies vary in complexity, and the charts in Appendix E show where using specific strategies is appropriate.

Frequently Misspelled Words

What good is teaching spelling if students aren't working on the words they misspell? Commonly misspelled words should have a prominent place in formal and informal spelling instruction. Lists from the Research in Action project of the hundred most commonly misspelled words at each grade level are included in Appendix C.

Where to Get Spelling Words

The primary source for finding words for spelling lists should be frequently misspelled words. You may want to collect lists of the words students in your class misspell so that you can truly customize your instruction, but, as with anything, use your best judgment. In Research in Action, words such as *teenage, mutant, ninja, turtle,* and *sewer* came up a lot. Students were using these words in their writing, but do you want to include them in formal spelling instruction?

Our list of the most commonly misspelled words for your grade level (see Appendix C) is a good source for spelling words, but please be aware of one small thing. You may think that it's a good idea to cover the list at your grade, and then cover the next grade's list too, to give your students a head start. If you try this you'll be disappointed. These lists are amazingly, but not surprisingly, similar across the grades.

Some secondary sources you may want to consider are lists of high frequency words in our language. These sources are available in most curriculum libraries, but you may need to write directly to the publishers to obtain some of them. In Appendix F you'll find a list of some sources you can use to find appropriate words for spelling instruction.

Where Not to Get Spelling Words

Knowing where not to get spelling list words is perhaps as important as knowing good sources for words. It's not a good idea to depend solely on basal reader or trade book vocabulary, content area vocabulary, or content area supplementary materials for words for spelling instruction. It's certainly acceptable to use these materials as a source to find words that may fit a spelling concept you are teaching, but spelling words should be related to one another by a spelling pattern, either sound, structure, or meaning. The vocabulary words in content area materials and basal readers are often too difficult for most children to spell. The rule of thumb is that spelling words should already be part of the children's vocabulary, especially for children in the lower grades. The process of learning spelling patterns of words is somewhat different from learning reading vocabulary. Vocabulary instruction is aimed at introducing children to new words. Spelling instruction should focus on helping students spell words they already know and use in their writing.

Conclusion

Direct spelling instruction certainly should be part of your language arts curriculum, regardless of your instructional approach. The Research in Action project confirmed that spelling should be taught in an organized fashion, with a logical progression of concept development and emphasis. A good spelling curriculum is multifaceted, covering sound patterns, rules and generalizations, spelling and meaning, developing spelling consciousness, strategies, and commonly misspelled words. Leaving any one of these elements out of your spelling curriculum is doing a disservice to your students. Don't rely on reading books and content area books to shape your spelling curriculum. A much more effective approach is to concentrate spelling instruction on children's developmental stages and the things they do when they misspell words. Putting together a spelling curriculum is a difficult, time-consuming task, but a well-designed, well-conceived spelling program is an essential part of an integrated language arts curriculum.

Kathryn Marine *is an Editor in the Integrated Language Arts Department at ScottForesman.*

Spelling Development:
Stages and Strategies

James Beers

A first-grade teacher looks over the stories that were written by her students in September and November. She notices that many words in the writing done in September did not contain vowel letters: for example, *kite* was spelled *kt*, rabbit was *rbt*, and *jungle gym* was *jgjm*. These and other words that appeared in the November writing, however, were spelled with appropriate vowel letters: *kite* became *kit* and *jungle gym* became *jogjim*. The teacher also noticed in the November writing that children were mistakenly ending many short vowel words with a final *e*. She attributed this error to the students' confusion between the short and long spelling, though she was surprised because they had worked on spelling long vowels for weeks.

In another classroom, a third-grade teacher who encourages invented spelling by students when they write is reading some of his students' latest writing efforts. He begins to feel overwhelmed by the large number of invented spellings in the writing. Two questions come into his mind when faced with so many misspelled words: *Where do I begin to help these students in spelling? How do I help them?*

A final spelling episode takes place in a fifth-grade classroom. Students are working in writing groups helping each other edit their science articles. The teacher walks over to one group and notices that one student has very few spelling errors. Another student in the same writing group, however, has numerous spelling errors, particularly with longer words. For example, *natural* is spelled *nacheril.* The teacher concludes that the student with fewer spelling errors is a better speller than the student with more spelling errors.

What do these episodes point out about students and spelling? Learning to spell is a long-term developmental process. Spelling research on students' spelling attempts over the past twenty years has identified developmental spelling stages (Read, 1975; Beers and Henderson, 1977; Henderson and Beers, 1980; Beers and Beers, 1981; Beers and Beers, 1991). These stages help to explain why the first graders left out vowel letters in their early spelling attempts and why the fifth grader spelled *natural* as *nacheril.* Recognizing spelling stages is especially important in classrooms where teachers encourage invented spelling because it helps those teachers make sense of misspellings. The third-grade teacher is likely to feel less overwhelmed by the number of invented spellings if the misspellings can be systematically identified and organized for instruction.

A developmental spelling perspective can also help to explain several misconceptions revealed in the classroom situations described above. One misconception is that first graders who end short vowel words with *e* are confusing short and long vowel spelling. Actually, it is quite normal for children to routinely overgeneralize from one spelling concept to another. For example, the first-grade children who started ending short vowel words, which they had previously spelled correctly, with silent *e* were learning about silent *e* in their reading and spelling programs. What they began to do with this new information was to incorrectly generalize it to old information. This explains why words such as *cost, stop,* and *run* began to appear as *coste, stope,* and *rune.* These young spellers were not necessarily confusing short and long vowels, but rather overgeneralizing the long vowel spelled with a silent *e* from long to short vowel words. Children learn best when they are allowed to make these kinds of developmentally appropriate mistakes.

Another misconception occurs in the fifth-grade spelling episode: Students who make few spelling errors in their writing are better spellers than students who make more spelling errors. In fact, students who have few spelling errors but also fewer polysyllabic words in their writing may not necessarily be better spellers than students who misspell polysyllabic words. The fifth grader who misspelled *natural* had spelled *nature* correctly in the same science article. This student may actually be a better speller than the other fifth grader but appears to have more spelling problems because she is attempting to write more difficult words than the other student. Once again, analyzing spelling errors from a developmental standpoint can give a much more accurate account of students' spelling abilities than simply looking at the number of spelling errors in their writing.

Prephonetic Spelling Stage

What are the developmental spelling stages? The earliest stage of spelling development, known as the prephonetic stage, actually begins long before children come to school. When very young children start to match words with meaning, their spelling development begins. Whether it's the EXXON sign that the three year old associates with gasoline or the KMART sign that the four year old links with toys, children's first impression is not of a word or even a group of related letters, but rather a meaningful visual sign or picture (Masonheimer, Drum, and Ehri, 1984).

As these children grow a little older, they begin to view written words as marks or squiggles on paper (Sulzby, Barnhart, and Hieshima, 1989). Sometimes these children will make marks, signs, or pictures on paper and arbitrarily assign meaning to them. When discussing their "writing," these children talk as if they are giving meaning to the marks (Dobson, 1989). As they grow more familiar with writing, letters or groups of letters begin to appear in and around the pictures or other signs on their papers.

By the time children reach the age of four or five, letters often begin to appear routinely in their "writing." The appearance of letters during this spelling stage indicates that a child is beginning to develop the concept of a written word (Morris and Perney, 1984). Initially this concept may be somewhat confused, with letters, numbers, and other marks appearing together in the same writing. Figure 1 is a first grader's account of a Fourth of July celebration. There are two lines of letters, some of which are repeated, but there is no relationship between the letters and what the child said was written.

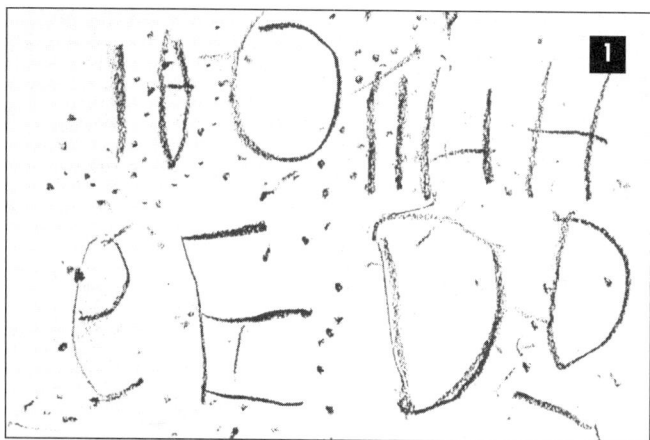

Figure 1: A first grader explains the letters and marks in his "writing": "We went to Yorktown to watch the fireworks on the Fourth of July. It was loud and had lots of colors. It was fun."

Sometimes a set of letters may be called a specific word one day and a different word another day. For example, a four year old wrote *xtrpppt* and called it *house* in one piece of writing, and then called it *caterpillar* in another piece of writing the next day. In other cases, children use the physical size or length of a collection of letters to convey meaning. For example, a five year old wrote *FFFFFFF* and *FFF* on a picture she had drawn. When asked to talk about her picture, she indicated that her dog had three puppies and that she had depicted the mother dog and her three puppies in the picture. The child wrote *FFFFFFFF* in large letters above the mother dog and three sets of *FFF* in much smaller letters next to three small puppy-looking figures. When asked about the letters, the child explained that the large mother dog needed a large word to identify her and the smaller puppies needed a smaller word. "You can tell she is the mother and they are her puppies," she concluded, "because the same letter is used in these words."

The following teaching suggestions will help prephonetic spellers develop the concept of a written word by establishing that there is a one-to-one correspondence between written and spoken words. The suggestions also will help students attend to initial- and final-consonant sounds.

- Read aloud and often. Use big books.
- Have students learn and use the alphabet song.
- Place alphabet strips on desks.
- Encourage students to draw and to "write."
- Use dictations and experience charts to show matches between spoken words and printed words.
- Have students echo- and choral-read dictations and poems.
- Play rhyming games.
- Put words around the room as labels for objects.
- Have students listen to and create pattern stories and poems.
- Begin picture sorts that focus on beginning sounds.
- Have students match picture cards with beginning consonants.
- Have students begin to develop picture/word banks.
- When beginning-consonant sorts are successful, move on to final-consonant sorts (pictures or words, depending on the student).

Early Phonetic Stage

As four and five year olds begin to learn the names of letters and even some of the sounds of letters, their spelling attempts start to attend to sounds in words that they want to write. Their spelling efforts at the *early phonetic stage* progress from using a single initial consonant to signify a word (*k* for *cat*), to using a single consonant letter followed by unrelated letters that act as place markers (*bsrsr* for *book*), to using first and last consonants for

---

words (*bk* for *bike, bsbl* for *baseball*), and, finally, to becoming aware that words have certain letters that stand for vowel sounds (*jop* for *jump, ronon* for *running*). During the early phonetic spelling stage, children begin to be able to segment or separate words into sound units that are represented by letters that approximate the sounds heard in the words (Beers and Beers, 1981; Morris, 1989). The words in children's writing at this stage begin to look more recognizable, as in Figures 2 through 4.

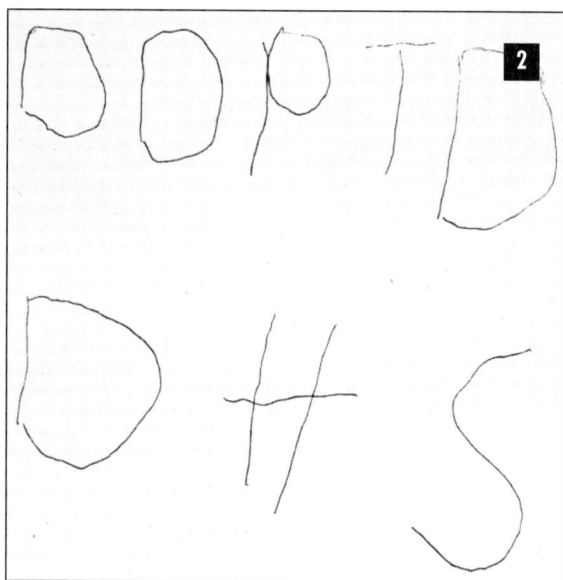

Figure 2: The child who wrote "Daddy painted the house" recognizes the phonetic relationship between the letters written and the sounds spoken.

Instructional strategies for early phonetic spellers should include activities that draw students' attention to the beginning, end, and middle of words, in that order:

- Focus on word families with different initial consonants.
- After initial-consonant word families, move on to final consonant word families.

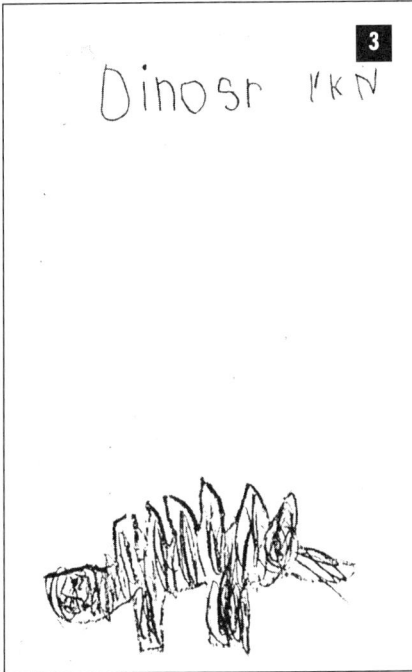

Figure 3: The young author of "Dinosaur walking" represents initial, middle, and final consonant sounds, and even some vowels.

Figure 4: This student's sentence says, "I like to go around the block with Kizzie." Notice how consistently consonants are spelled and how often vowels are omitted.

- Begin consonant-blend picture/word sorts.
- Begin contrasting consonant/consonant-blend word sorts.
- Begin short-vowel picture/word sorts.
- Begin consonant-digraph word sorts.
- Begin contrasting consonant/consonant-digraph word sorts.

Phonetic Spelling Stage

As children in kindergarten, first grade, or second grade begin to read and write, they move more firmly into the *phonetic spelling stage.* Their spelling is characterized by the use of letter names for short vowel sounds (*et* for *it*), the omission of silent *e* with long vowel sounds (*hop* for *hope, slep* for *sleep*), and the inclusion of phonetically spelled endings (*askt* for *asked, skard* for *scared, savd* for *saved, techiz* for *teachers*). Since children at this level of spelling development can represent any word phonetically when they write, they often become very prolific writers. It is not unusual for phonetic spellers in the first grade to create stories that fill five to ten pages of primary paper. Figures 5 though 8 show student writing at the phonetic spelling stage.

To help phonetic spellers recognize the differences between short- and long-vowel spellings and the spelling of common word endings, try the following kinds of activities:

- Have students do long-vowel picture/word sorts.
- Have students do short/long-vowel word sorts.
- Have students do vowel-blend word sorts.
- Encourage students to use their best phonetic spelling.
- Have students develop personal dictionaries.
- Have students identify their own "problem" words.
- Have students act as spelling editors for each other.

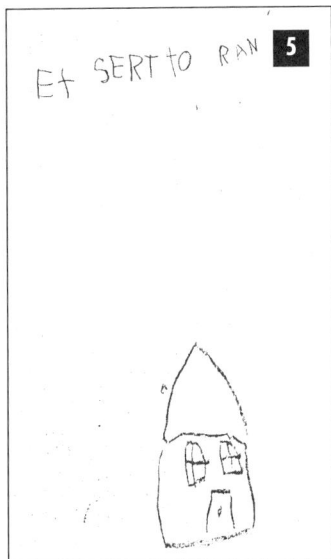

Figure 5: While most single consonant sounds are spelled accurately, the second letter of a consonant blend or digraph is often omitted. Here, the *t* is missing from the blend at the beginning of *started.*

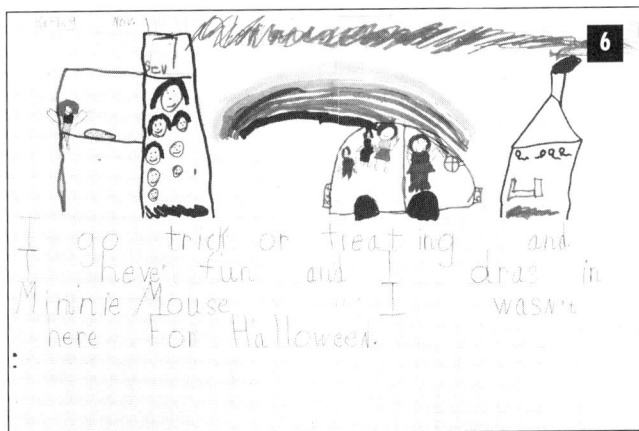

Figure 6: Letter names are often used because they sound like the sounds being spelled. Here letter name *a* is used for short *e* in *dress.*

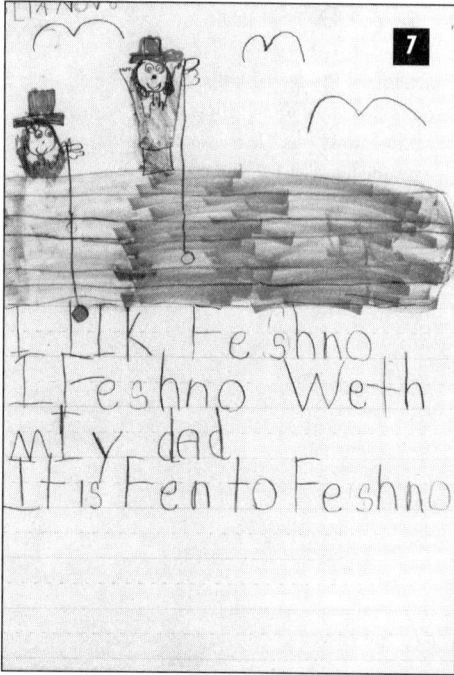

Figure 7: Long vowels frequently appear without final *e,* as with *lik* for *like.*

I LIK Feshno
I Feshno Weth
MIy dad
It is Fen to Feshno

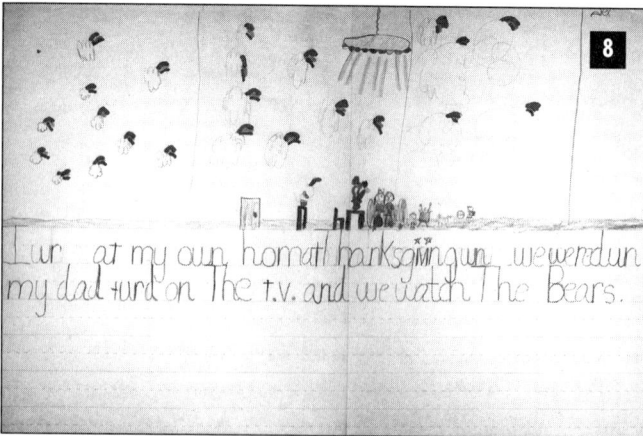

I wr at my aun homatl harksgiving un we wer dun my dad turd on The t.v. and we watch The Bears.

Figure 8: Endings are often spelled phonetically at this stage, as with *turd* for *turned.*

Structural Spelling Stage

The next stage along the spelling development continuum is the *structural spelling stage.* Children usually reach this stage by late second grade or early third grade. Spelling at this level is characterized by correct spellings of words with short vowels and common endings. Misspellings of long-vowel words persist, but the most common misspellings at this stage typically occur at the point where the last syllable in a root word meets a subsequent ending (Beers and Beers, 1991). For example, students seem to have difficulty deciding when to double or not double a consonant, writing words such as *havving* for *having, spining* for *spinning,* or *separatting* for *separating.* Another very common error is misspelling schwa sounds in unaccented syllables: for example, *butin* for *button.* Figures 9 through 11 show common errors of the structural spelling stage.

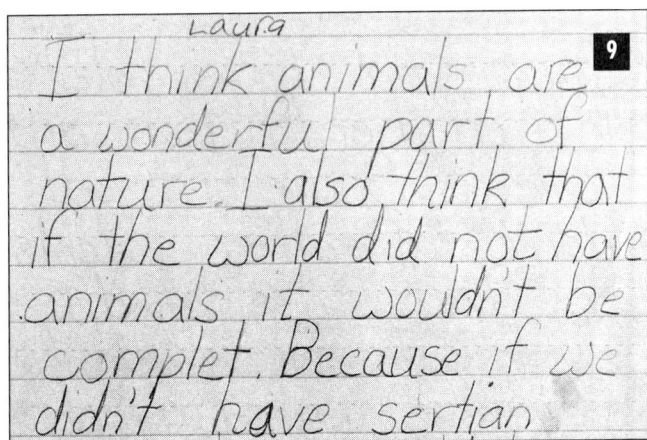

Laura

I think animals are a wonderful part of nature. I also think that if the world did not have animals it wouldn't be complet. Because if we didn't have sertian

Figure 9: At the structural stage, short vowels are often spelled correctly, but long-vowel spellings remain problematic. For example, here the final *e* is omitted from *complete.*

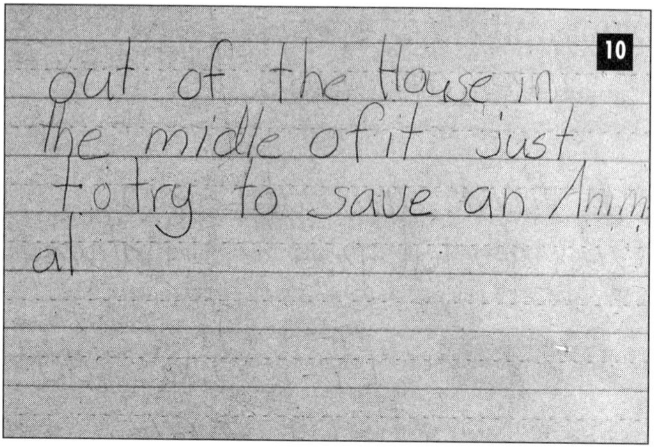

out of the Hause in
the midle of it just
to try to save an Anim
al

Figure 10: This student made the common error of not doubling the consonant in *middle*.

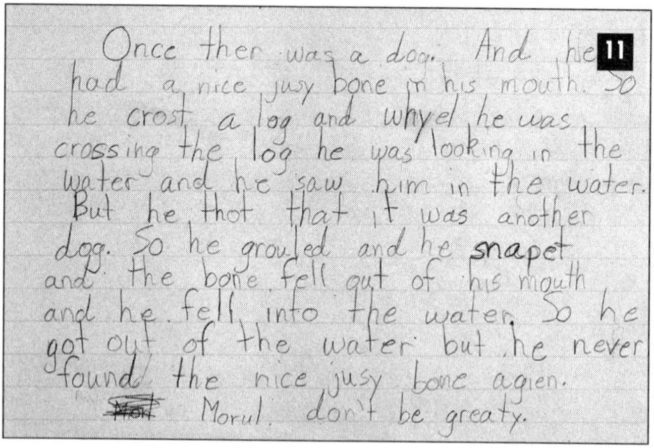

Once ther was a dog. And he
had a nice jusy bone in his mouth. So
he crost a log and whyel he was
crossing the log he was looking in the
water and he saw him in the water.
But he thot that it was another
dog. So he grouled and he snapet
and the bone fell out of his mouth
and he fell into the water. So he
got out of the water but he never
found the nice jusy bone agien.
Morul, don't be greaty.

Figure 11: This student is still having problems with long vowels, consonants, and schwas: *greaty* for *greedy*, *morul* for *moral*.

Students at the structural spelling stage begin to realize that phonetic spelling can help them with many parts of many words. However, there are other structural features in words that are not affected by sound. To help structural spellers move to the next developmental stage, offer activities such as these:

- Review common structural elements in words.
- Begin one- and two-syllable word sorts with endings.
- Review common consonant and vowel patterns with word sorts.
- Do word sorts with endings without root change.
- Do word sorts with endings with root change.
- Do word sorts with double consonants within the root.
- Do final-schwa-syllable word sorts.
- Do schwa-vowel word sorts (other syllables).

Meaning/Derivational Spelling Stage

Finally, in about the fourth or fifth grade, students who have progressed through the spelling stages we have discussed reach the important *meaning/derivational* stage of spelling development (DeHaven, 1988). By this time, doubling errors have begun to decrease, but students continue to misspell phonetically alternate forms of words they spell correctly, as with *admeration* and *admire.* This phenomenon is also illustrated in the example given earlier about the fifth grader who spelled *nature* correctly but misspelled *natural* as *nacheril.* As they progress, students learn that the spelling of root words helps in spelling their alternate forms.

It should come as no surprise that students frequently make errors when attempting to spell these difficult alternate forms, or forms derived from Latin or Greek. Students who have written and read widely through their elementary school years often use more advanced words in their writing and are, therefore, sometimes more likely to make spelling errors. To help meaning/derivational spellers understand the relationships among words, suggest the activities on the following page.

- Have students do word-expansion activities: *happy, happier, unhappy, happily, happiest.*
- Have students do word sorts that connect spelling changes in words: related words with no root change *(nation/national)*, related words with silent letters *(sign/signal)*, and related words that have spelling changes *(promote/promotion, explore/exploration, mature/maturity).*
- Have students sort related words that change from short to long forms *(ignite/ignition).*
- Have students sort related words that change from long vowel sound to schwa *(invite/invitation).*
- Have students sort related words that change from schwa to short vowel sound *(central/centrality)*
- Have students do common Latin/Greek word sorts.
- Have students create meaning maps using derived/related forms.
- Have students do word etymologies for spelling and meaning.

When students have successfully passed through the meaning/derivational spelling stage, they recognize that English spelling has three important features: sound, structure, and meaning. They learn that pronunciation is often linked to the structural elements in words and reflected in their spelling, and that even when pronunciation and/or structure are changed in a word, the spelling of the word remains recognizable in its alternate or derived forms.

James Beers *is a Professor of Reading and Language Arts at the College of William and Mary in Williamsburg, Virginia.*

The Spelling and Meaning Connection:
Another Dimension

W. Dorsey Hammond

Why Are Words Spelled As They Are?

Many words are quite predictable in their spelling. Often we can spell such words correctly even when we have never seen them before. Other words aren't so predictable. When spelling such words, we're never quite sure whether they end in *-ary, -ory,* or *-ery,* whether the consonant is double or single, or whether the unaccented syllable is spelled with an *a, e, i, o,* or *u.* Then there are truly bewildering words such as *yacht, aisle, debut, buoy,* and *rhythm.*

On the surface, spelling sometimes looks haphazard or random. In fact, the more research we do on spelling, the more evidence there is that the English spelling system is more predictable and rational than originally believed. Two important areas of research have enlightened us about the spelling process.

In a classic work, Hanna, Hanna, Hodges, and Rudorf (1965) analyzed almost every word in the English language and found surprising regularity in spelling patterns. One interesting factor in their analysis was the position of letters in words. For example, the letters *gh* represent the sound /f/ only when positioned at the end of a word, as in *laugh, rough,* and *tough.* When *gh* is at the beginning of a word, however, it always represents the sound /g/, as in *ghost.* In another example, the letters *ti,* representing the sound /sh/, occur only when followed by *on,* as in *lotion, motion,* and *nation.*

The other important line of spelling research, conducted primarily by Henderson (1977, 1992) and his colleagues over the last twenty-five years, is particularly enlightening. Inspired by the seminal work of Charles Read (1971) in his investigation of young children's spelling from age three to six, Henderson and his graduate students at the University of Virginia began analyzing children's developmental, or invented, spellings. After more than a hundred independent studies over a twenty-five-year period, several irrefutable findings emerged.

1. Spelling is developmental: As young people mature in the early years of school, spelling improves.
2. Young children's opportunities to experiment with the spelling system and to invent their own spellings hasten spelling achievement.
3. Children's invented spellings are highly predictable and consistent, suggesting an underlying cognitive and linguistic system from which children generate their approximate and invented spellings, as well as their conventional spellings.

The combined research of Hanna and colleagues and Henderson and colleagues gives us major insights into how spelling works and how a curriculum for spelling can be developed. Hanna and colleagues (1966) showed how words are spelled. Henderson and colleagues (1980, 1992) showed how children learn to spell the conventional patterns that Hanna described. Indeed the research of invented spellings is arguably among the most enlightening research in language arts in the latter half of this century. Nevertheless, there are areas of spelling still to be discovered. Since much of Henderson's work addressed spelling by children in the primary grades, there is room for more spelling research focusing on older children.

Templeton (1983, 1992) has begun to turn his attention to the spelling of older students in the intermediate and middle school grades. His findings suggest that spelling researchers and curriculum specialists need to expand their investigation beyond that of phonology (sounds) and grapheme (letter) relationships to focus on other factors that may contribute to spelling proficiency.

Other recent research supports Templeton's findings, indicating that there is more of a meaning base to spelling than was previously believed. For example, a student may wonder why *meant,* as in "I meant to do it," is not spelled *ment,* like *rent* and *sent,* until she is reminded that *meant* is the past tense of *mean.* Since *mean* is spelled with *ea,* it makes sense that *meant* is spelled similarly. In another example, a child may question why the word *health* isn't spelled *helth* until he is reminded that its base word is *heal.* When we look at these words on the basis of a letter-sound relationship, their spellings seem phonetically irregular. However, these spellings are quite rational when we examine them on the basis of meaning or grammar.

Can Meaning Connections Aid Spelling?

Are there many words whose spelling can be determined or predicted on the basis of a meaning connection and, if so, does this have implications for spelling instruction? The answer to the first part of the question is a qualified yes. There does appear to be a sizable number of words whose spellings can be explained on the basis of meaning, morphology, and/or grammar. However, no systematic, definitive study has been conducted to determine how and to what extent meaning relates to spelling. Most of the work on this subject is anecdotal and selective. Although Templeton's (1992) work makes an important contribution, further long-term investigation about the meaning-spelling connection is needed.

If the spelling of words does indeed have a significant meaning connection, the answer to the second part of the question is a resounding yes: There would be important instructional and curricular implications. Good spellers probably use meaning-based and morphological strategies intuitively; however, for most students, instruction in spelling strategies is necessary in order to improve spelling performance.

The research of Cramer and Cipielewski (1995), in which more than 1,500,000 words were analyzed for patterns of spelling errors, provides an important data base for examining any meaning connection to spelling. The words in the study originated from approximately 19,000 samples of writing by children in grades 1–8. Cramer's preliminary analysis supports the findings of Templeton that there are spelling patterns that are predictable on the basis of meaning or morphology. Cramer's analysis addresses three points about the relationship between spelling and meaning.

1. Words with an underlying meaning connection often provide clues for spelling related words, as with *politics* and *political* or *realize* and *realization.* Often the related words are presented in a different grammatical form, as in the examples above, or a tense change produces a spelling change, as with *mean* and *meant* or *hear* and *heard.*

2. Meaning or language usage aids spelling in additional ways. Many spelling errors in grades 1–8 are actually errors in usage, as in words such as *their, there,* and *they're.* Spelling is dictated by the use of the word in context. Knowing that *they're* is a contraction for *they are* aids in spelling *they're* correctly. Basic Latin and Greek derivatives aid in spelling words such as *bicycle, biplane,* and *biannual.* Base, or root, words also can aid in correct spelling, as in *govern* and *government.*

3. Not often discussed is the notion that spelling patterns give clues to the meaning of unknown words. In many cases, students may speculate about the meaning of an unknown word based on a simpler known form, as in *medicine* and *medicinal* or *mechanic, mechanical,* and *mechanization.*

Correct spelling provides little or no margin for error. Put simply, in order to spell a word correctly, one has to spell every element within the word correctly. Parts of almost any word are easy to spell. Other elements within a given word may be much more difficult to predict. As teachers of spelling, we need to focus on the portions of words that present the highest probability of being misspelled. For example, in unknown spelling situations, spellers often wonder whether to use *c* or *s*, whether the schwa sound should be represented by *a, e, i, o,* or *u,* or whether to use the ending -*ar* (as in *dollar*), -*er* (as in *farmer*), or -*or* (as in *doctor*). One teaching method is to simply have students memorize common troublesome spellings. A far more promising alternative, however, is to help students develop strategies to determine correct spellings and reduce the load on rote memory.

Variant Forms Aid Spelling

As suggested earlier, one strategy that has not received enough attention in spelling programs is using other forms of a word to determine the word's correct spelling. For example, assume a sixth-grade student is attempting to spell the word *strategy*. The troublesome spot is probably the second syllable, which is unaccented. The likely question the speller asks is whether it should be an *a,* as in *realize;* an *e,* as in *elephant;* an *i,* as in *medicine;* and so on. However, if the speller thinks of the word *strategic,* a strong sound clue is provided that the letter *e* should be written to represent the vowel in the second syllable of *strategy.* Conversely, if the speller is unsure of the vowel spelling in the first syllable of *strategic,* the first syllable of *strategy* provides a strong indication of the letter *a.* These two examples illustrate how a different form of the same word can provide valuable information about correct spelling.

Table 1 shows examples of how knowledge of one word can help in spelling a related word.

Table 1
Spelling Using Related Words

policy	politics	political
memory	memorial	memorize
muscle	muscular	
realize	realization	
organize	organization	
colony	colonial	
compete	competition	
minor	minority	
major	majority	
obey	obedient	
resign	resignation	
combine	combination	

It is possible to determine how to spell the troublesome schwa sounds in *policy, realization, competition,* and *combination,* for example, by thinking of the words *political, realize, compete,* and *combine,* respectively. (In many parts of Canada, *organization* and *realization* are pronounced with the long *i* in the third syllable, thus facilitating the correct spelling of these words.) In the word *major,* the long *a* spelling is a helpful clue in figuring out how to spell the first vowel in *majority.* In some dialects, the spelling of the second syllable in *major* is aided by knowledge of the spelling of the second syllable in *majority.* The spelling of *muscle* makes more sense when one thinks of the modified form *muscular.*

In summary, there is ample evidence that a related form of a target word may aid in its spelling. Admittedly the strategy doesn't always work. Some words change spelling and pronunciation when they change form: *pronounce* and *pronunciation, renounce* and *renunciation, maintain* and *maintenance, repeat* and *repetition.* In most cases, the pronunciation change helps retain phonetic regularity. The strategy appears to be more applicable for students of the upper-elementary and middle school grades and beyond. Also, one needs an extensive and flexible vocabulary to make the system work well. It is likely that good spellers use this strategy intuitively. For less able spellers, teaching such a strategy in spelling instruction would most likely be very helpful because it enables them to make sense of spelling situations without having to rely on memorization.

Meaning Aids Spelling

As stated earlier, meaning may make more of a contribution to spelling than previously acknowledged. Most everyone is familiar with words such as *breakfast*, meaning to *break* the *fast*, and *cupboard*, meaning a *board* for *cups*. Latin and Greek derivatives are meaning-based and provide spelling clues in related words such as *trio, tricycle, triple*, and *triangle; quart, quarter, quartet*, and *quartile; monorail, monologue, monocle*, and *monopoly*; and *astronomy, astronaut*, and *astrology*. In Table 2 are additional examples of words with a strong meaning connection that can aid in spelling.

Table 2
Meaning Connections That Aid Spelling

union	unit	unite	unison
minimum	minimal	miniature	mini-store
obey	obedient	obedience	
memory	memorial	memorize	
sign	signature		
resign	resignation		
receipt	receive		
magnify	magnificent		
volume	voluminous		
hymn	hymnal		
labor	laboratory		
condemn	condemnation		

Another meaning-based spelling pattern involves root, or base, words. In the Cramer and Cipielewski (1995) study, intermediate grade and middle school students often misspell *government* as *goverment*, deleting the letter *n*. They also misspell *Christmas* as *Chrismas*, deleting the letter *t*. In both cases, attention to the base words, *govern* and *Christ*, would help eliminate such errors.

Compund words such as *sisters-in-law* or *attorneys general* often cause spelling problems. Adolescent and adult spellers often write these words as *sister-in-laws* or *attorney generals*. Explaining that the compound words refer to the *sisters* and *attorneys*, not the *laws* and *generals*, can help students avoid making these common mistakes.

Many students have usage problems with homophones such as *here* and *hear; there, their* and *they're;* and *to, too,* and *two.* The best way to correct these spelling problems is through teacher explanation and modeling. Teachers may encourage students to use mnemonic devices or specific strategies to help them use homophones appropriately:

- The number 2 is written as <u>*two*</u> and begins like the word <u>*twice*</u>.
- The word *too* means also or in <u>*addition*</u>, so <u>*add*</u> another <u>*o*</u>.
- A place with *there* or *where* always includes *here*.
- *Hear* means "to listen" because it includes the word *ear*.

Spelling Aids Meaning

We have examined numerous examples of how meaning aids spelling. Many of these examples can be used to show that the reverse is also true—spelling aids meaning. Put another way, how a word is spelled may give clues about its meaning.

Assume a fourth- or fifth-grade student is reading and encounters the following sentence: "She was a *humane* person, always caring for others." The word *humane* is a "new" word for this young reader. Clearly context helps with the meaning, but, in addition, the reader notices that the word *humane* looks very much like the word *human*. He hypothesizes that *humane* must have something to do with being *human*.

In another example of spelling giving clues about meaning, a tenth-grade student reads about an individual having *malevolent* tendencies. The word *malevolent* is a "new" word for her. At first, she hypothesizes that *malevolent* has something to do with being male. However, in subsequent sentences, words such as *evil, greed,* and *mistreatment* appear in the description of the *malevolent* character. She also notices that the word looks very much like a word she recently learned, *malady,* and she remembers that in discussions by adults she has heard the word *malignant* used in a negative context. Thus she begins to build a theory that *malevolent* must refer to ill feelings, bad behavior, and so on. Conversely the word *benevolent* seems to be a more positive term because it reminds her of the word *benefit* and because recently she heard that the tumor of her neighbor was fortunately *benign,* not *malignant.* Here again, the spelling pattern, along with context, provides clues to meaning.

Spelling patterns involving roots and derivatives often provide useful information about the meaning of words. For example, a student who encounters *quartile* for the first time knows that it is similar to *quart, quarter, quartet,* and *square,* which all have to do with four or one-fourth. Thus the student determines that *quartile* refers to the concept of fourths in some way. In Table 3 are examples of spelling patterns involving roots and derivatives that can offer clues about word meaning and, thereby, contribute to vocabulary growth.

Table 3
Meaning-Related Words

resolve	resolute	resolution
obey	obedient	obedience
example	exemplary	exemplify
reside	residential	residence
colony	colonial	colonialism
unit	unanimous	unanimity
similar	simile	facsimile
habit	habitual	habitat

These examples describe how vocabulary grows. The point here is twofold. First, learners make inferences about word meaning not unlike the inferences made in the comprehension of text. Second, students can draw on two major sources to hypothesize or confirm the meaning of a word: context and spelling patterns. Educators have understood the role of context for many years; however, we have paid very little attention to the role of spelling patterns. Apparently students haven't either. In an unpublished study, Templeton and Barone (1989) found that fifth-, sixth-, and seventh-grade students acknowledged that vocabulary could help spelling but saw little possibility that spelling could facilitate vocabulary growth.

Conclusion

In summary, the insights we have gained from spelling research have important implications for instruction. First, it is likely that students who have good vocabularies and strong language facility already make spelling and meaning connections intuitively. However, for most students, it is important that these connections between spelling and meaning, and meaning and spelling, be taught and discussed in school. Second, the more spelling strategies, both phonetic and meaning, we can provide students, the less they will need to rely on memorization techniques. Finally, as we develop spelling curriculum for the twenty-first century, we need to consider grouping words not only by phonetic patterns but by meaning patterns as well.

W. Dorsey Hammond *is a Professor of Education at Oakland University in Rochester, Michigan.*

Making Better Spellers:
Integrating Spelling, Reading, and Writing

Ronald L. Cramer

Reading and writing are natural allies of spelling in the acquisition of spelling competence. This article explores reading and writing as they relate to spelling in an integrated language arts teaching approach. It is organized into the following four parts: (1) introduction (2) spelling and reading, (3) spelling, reading, and writing, and (4) integrating language arts.

Introduction

Anyone who has been in education for any length of time knows that teaching theories come into vogue and they go out of vogue. However, some theories do return, evolve, improve, and stay around. The current Whole Language approach to teaching evolved from the Language Experience teaching theories, whose major proponents included E. B. Huey, Sylvia Ashton-Warner, John Dewey, Russell Stauffer, and Roach Van Allen. Both teaching approaches, Whole Language and Language Experience, embody a number of important ideas about language acquisition and literacy:

1. Language, whether oral or written, is best learned in meaningful social contexts.
2. Language arts instruction, particularly reading and writing, should be integrated.
3. Language is acquired and retained through meaningful use and practice.
4. Language is easiest to learn when it is presented whole rather than in isolated pieces.
5. Language instruction should focus on the individual language and experience of the learner.

Although educators differ in their beliefs about how to interpret and implement these basic theories, many agree on their relevance to literacy instruction. As educators, we can only benefit from shifting our focus from the differences that divide us to the similarities that bring us together, as Stanovich (1994) and Church (1994) have thoughtfully suggested in recent articles in *The Reading Teacher*. The principles of Whole Language and Language Experience point the way toward an integrated reading-writing approach that can surmount the spelling obstacle. And make no mistake, spelling is a major obstacle to approaching literacy through reading and writing.

Spelling and Reading

For millions of American children, Noah Webster's blue-backed speller prevailed for a hundred years as the principal means of learning to read and spell. For centuries before that, spelling drill dominated as the primary method of teaching reading (Adams, 1990). Were our ancestors simply ill informed, or were they acting on the valid premise that reading strengthens spelling and spelling strengthens reading? Ancient folk wisdom and modern research both support the idea that there is indeed a reciprocal relationship between learning to read and learning to spell. Sixty years ago, Arthur Gates (1936) found a strong reciprocal relationship between reading and spelling. Research conducted since Gates's investigation has confirmed his early insight (Betts, 1945; Templin, 1954; Rudisell, 1957; Morrison and Perry, 1959; Plessas and Ladley, 1963; Cramer, 1968, 1971; Chomsky, 1971; Stauffer et al., 1972; Ehri, 1984; Ehri and Wilce, 1987; Henderson, 1989; Templeton, 1989; Templeton and Bear, 1992).

Reading Aids Spelling. An ancient Chinese proverb says, "The reading of 10,000 books produces a magic pen." Perhaps this ancient wisdom may be extended to say, "The reading of 10,000 books produces a skilled speller." Reading provides essential background information about letters, sounds, meaning, and word structure, each of which plays an important role in spelling. The richer the base of linguistic knowledge acquired through reading, the greater the likelihood that good spelling will result. This is not to say that reading guarantees good spelling; there are good readers who are poor spellers. However, these individuals are the exception rather than the rule. Although reading proficiency is not a sufficient explanation for spelling competence, it is certainly a significant factor in spelling competence.

Spelling Aids Reading. If reading strengthens spelling, how does spelling aid reading? Research shows that phonological awareness, or the ability to analyze and segment sounds within words, is highly correlated with later success in learning to read. Ball and Blachman (1991) investigated the effects of training in phonemic segmentation and instruction in letter names and letter sounds on kindergarten children's reading and spelling skills. Results indicated that phonemic awareness training, combined with instruction connecting the phonemic segments to alphabet letters, significantly improved the early reading and spelling skills of the children in the study. The relationship between learning to read and learning to spell is particularly pronounced among children in the primary grades (Blachman, 1984; Stanovich, Cunningham, and Cramer, 1984; Cramer, 1985; Bradley and Bryant, 1985; Juel, Griffith, and Gough, 1986; Mann and Liberman, 1984.)

How to deliver phonemic awareness training is an important concern, especially for teachers oriented toward the Language Experience and Whole Language approaches. Ayres (1993) found that direct instruction in phonemic awareness produced its most significant effect after a foundation of literature had been provided. Children reconstructed stories, using feltboard cutouts, after listening to literature read aloud. This sequence of instruction produced greater gains in phonemic awareness than direct instruction followed by story reconstruction.

Importance of Word Study. Word study is another essential of effective spelling and reading instruction (Henderson and Beers, 1980; Henderson and Templeton, 1986; Henderson, 1989; Cunningham and Allington, 1994). The purpose of word study is not merely to learn rules and patterns that determine spelling, but to instill a habit of examining words. What is learned through word study also enriches reading knowledge and writing skills. Word study activities should focus on the three basic features of words: (1) sound, (2) structure, and (3) meaning.

In early spelling development, familiarity with letter-sound correspondences and spelling patterns is essential to the development of spelling skills. Instruction in phonics and word analysis facilitates the development of spelling proficiency. Instruction in spelling patterns of vowels and consonants enables children to "teach themselves" in new spelling situations. Spelling pattern instruction has its greatest influence on children in the primary grades.

Particular emphasis should be given to structure instruction in the intermediate elementary grades. Word-structure rules determine how words are affected when inflected endings and affixes are added. The more children know about the logic of word structure, the more they are able to adapt in new spelling situations. Children acquire linguistic information most successfully by encountering language in natural reading and writing situations rather than by learning specific rules. Linguistic knowledge and command of the rules that govern spelling are learned by using language for meaningful purposes rather than by rote memorization.

For example, suppose you want children to learn how base words change when different endings are added. You could teach the formal rule for doubling final consonants when an ending is added, or you could provide children with a set of words that are examples of the rule, such as *hop—hopped* and *grab—grabbed,* and nonexamples of the rule, such as *hope—hoped* and *play—played,* and have them sort the words into appropriate categories. You might start by classifying the words yourself, and then have the children sort the words. With sufficient practice, children will begin to discover how doubling final consonants works when various suffixes are added.

Although Noah Webster's drill methods of instruction were lacking, he was correct to conclude that reading and spelling work together to strengthen language skills. The current Whole Language approach to teaching language arts utilizes the reciprocity between spelling and reading, helping students strengthen their spelling knowledge through reading and their reading knowledge through spelling.

Spelling, Reading, and Writing

Writing is crucial to an integrated approach to literacy. Emphasizing writing early adds enormous power to beginning reading, writing, and spelling instruction. How can children best learn the written language? The traditional approach has been to teach reading first and later teach writing and spelling. Chomsky (1979) believes this approach is inadequate, since it does not provide enough opportunity to produce language for personal and meaningful purposes.

> For maximum effectiveness, school instruction should begin with
> writing and progress to reading, as an outgrowth of abilities
> developed through experience with inventing one's own spellings
> (p. 43).

Chomsky is surely correct in her assessment of the importance of beginning writing early. One might quibble as to whether writing precedes reading in the technical sense, but this quibble would miss the larger, valid point that Chomsky makes concerning the nature of the tasks involved in writing and their contribution to the development of literacy. This writer believes writing and reading should begin simultaneously in an integrated, natural fashion, based on the principles of Language Experience and Whole Language teaching approaches.

The beneficial reciprocity between spelling and reading is further enhanced when reading and writing are taught in unison rather than as isolated activities. Reading provides linguistic information useful for writing, and writing provides linguistic information useful for reading. As reading and writing skills develop, spelling knowledge follows. Chomsky (1971) emphasizes the importance of providing a meaning-based reading curriculum to facilitate the benefits of integrating reading, writing, and spelling:

> Children are well equipped to organize linguistic knowledge on the basis of rich and varied inputs, to seek regularities, and to construct tacit rule systems. What they need in reading, beyond the requisite background, is adequate input of understood text (p. 54).

This reciprocal cycle of linguistic enrichment is forcefully demonstrated in research on invented spelling. Such research shows that children who have ample opportunity to write using their own invented spellings during their early school experience quickly acquire crucial information about spelling patterns, relationships between letters and sounds, spelling-meaning connections, and word-structure patterns.

Cramer (1968, 1970) conducted one of the earliest investigations of the influence of invented spelling on reading and writing achievement. Piggy-backing Russell Stauffer's first-grade reading project, Cramer investigated the effects of a Language Experience approach versus a Basal Reader approach on the spelling achievement of children in first grade. Children who received the Language Experience approach were taught to write independently, using their own invented spelling. Within six months, many of these children could produce some independent writing; by June, most of them demonstrated exceptional spelling competence. The level of spelling competence of the Language Experience group was startling when compared with that of the Basal Reader group. The Language Experience students

- spelled words better and sooner than their counterparts when writing connected discourse;

- spelled regular and irregular words better than their counterparts;
- spelled irregular words as well as they spelled regular words, whereas their counterparts had particular difficulty with irregular words;
- accurately produced significant parts of unknown words, whereas their counterparts did not;
- became better readers and writers than their counterparts; and
- still exhibited an advanced level of competence when tested three years later and again six years later at the conclusion of Stauffer's longitudinal study (Stauffer and Hammond, 1969; Stauffer, Hammond, Oehlkers, and Houseman, 1972).

Integrating Language Arts

It is true that the teaching of reading, writing, and spelling requires different, specific instructional strategies; however, integrating all three in a language arts program can have highly effective results. English spelling is complex and requires years to fully master. Yet we have learned that children can approximate correct spelling at a very early age and that this facility provides the keys to the kingdom of literacy.

Encourage invented spelling. Writing can be initiated much earlier than had been previously supposed (Cramer, 1968; Read, 1970, 1971; Chomsky, 1971; Bissex, 1980; Clark, 1989). When children use their knowledge of letters and sounds to approximate the spelling of a word they do not know, they are temporarily inventing its spelling. Invented spelling enables children to use their existing background of word knowledge to write partially correct spellings of words that they have not yet learned to spell correctly. Writing with invented spelling may be the best way to increase children's functional knowledge of letters and sounds (Cramer, 1985; Stanovich, 1988; Mann, Tobin, and Wilson, 1988; Clark, 1989; Housel, 1989; Moriarty, 1990). Invented spelling combines practice in letter formation, phonemic awareness, and letter-sound relationships, while enabling children to engage in the construction of meaningful ideas as they write stories, poems, personal essays, and reports.

Early invented misspellings are not retained in mature spelling, just as the early mispronunciations of a three-year-old child are not retained in mature speech. On the contrary, early invented spellings are stepping stones to correct spelling, as are early mispronunciations as young children acquire oral language. Children have a better chance of learning the rules and patterns that govern written language when they are surrounded by a rich print environment and are encouraged to explore it through meaningful learning experiences.

Focus on meaning. It is important for children, and teachers, to understand that the mechanics of writing, such as spelling and grammar, are vehicles for expressing ideas. Although learning the mechanics of writing is important, it is secondary to learning how to express ideas clearly in writing. During the early stages of learning to spell, young writers often find themselves overwhelmed with the problem of matching letters to sounds. If the spelling must be correct, the meaning and the message will inevitably suffer. Invented spelling helps children focus their attention on the message rather than on the mechanics of writing. As children gradually acquire a spelling vocabulary, their fluency as writers will grow naturally.

Writing moves through stages from initial draft to final product. First-draft writing should emphasize the fluent expression of ideas, while temporarily placing less emphasis on the spelling and other mechanics of writing. The editing-proofreading stage of writing is the right time to check words for correct spelling. Of course, not all pieces of writing reach this stage, and due consideration must be given to the experience and ability of the writer. As writing progresses toward the editing-proofreading stage, opportunities arise to apply strategies for checking spelling accuracy. The strategies needed to check spelling can be taught. For example, classroom spelling charts, conferencing with peers, conferencing with the teacher, and systematic spelling instruction help develop spelling knowledge that can be applied during the editing-proofreading stage.

Teach spelling. Spelling develops best in an environment in which there is exposure to literature, frequent independent reading, opportunity for personal writing, and systematic spelling instruction. Spelling instruction should concentrate on teaching a basic spelling vocabulary. If a basic spelling vocabulary is not established, children will not have a sufficient base on which to build new spelling knowledge.

Children need instruction in spelling starting in first grade and continuing through high school. Incidental exposure to reading and writing alone will not suffice for most children. Spelling instruction requires time, about forty to sixty minutes each week. It requires meaningful activities for learning words and developing a spelling conscience. It requires systematic study of a well-researched list of words. And, finally, it requires integrated language arts instruction, where the connections between reading, writing, and spelling are manifest.

In conclusion, writing engages the individual in the task of producing meaning, while reading engages the reader in the process of sharing, interpreting, and reacting to the ideas and experiences of the writer. Reading and writing form the foundations of literacy, and spelling proficiency is essential to both. Given the right sort of classroom experiences, children not only manage the task of learning to spell, they thrive on it.

Ronald L. Cramer *is a Professor of Education and Chairman of the Department of Reading and Language Arts at Oakland University in Rochester, Michigan.*

Appendix A:

Participating Teachers in the Research in Action Project

Ora Abdur-Razzaq
  Brooklyn, New York
Suzanne Addington,
  McRoberts, Kentucky
Connie Addis
  Walhalla, South Carolina
Anne Marie Agostinelli
  West Seneca, New York
Jeani Allphin
  Mounds, Oklahoma
Carolyn Ambler
  West Chester, Pennsylvania
Denise Amrhein
  Clifton Park, New York
Lucia Anderson
  Palm Bay, Florida
Heather Anderton
  Norcross, Georgia
Madelyn Andre
  Walls, Mississippi
Phyllis Andrus
  Ferron, Utah
Maryann Artesani
  Warwick, Rhode Island
Joan Arundale
  Warwick, Rhode Island
Karen Baines
  Louisville, Kentucky
Marie Barnhart
  Heavener, Oklahoma
Doris Barrett
  Hinesville, Georgia

Georgiana Barrett
  Jacksonville, Florida
Kristine Barrett
  Abilene, Kansas
Bessie Barrigai
  Montour Fall, New York
Kathleen Beaumont
  Walhalla, South Carolina
Carol Bednarowski
  Manchester, New Hampshire
Cathy Beemer
  Chapel Hill, North Carolina
Stephanie Bennett
  Covington, Louisiana
Maryann Bice
  York, South Carolina
Dorinda Bichham
  Van Cleave, Mississippi
Linda Biernat
  Montgomery, Alabama
Dorothy Bilodeau
  Auburn, Maine
Joyce Black
  Winslow, Maine
Rebecca Black
  Jacksonville, Florida
Marsha Block
  Houston, Texas
Marilyn Bodnar
  Lakewood, California
Sandie Boldt
  Sidney, Montana

Julie Bolyer
Shreveport, Louisiana

Deborah Bonner
Ft. Worth, Texas

Mary Bradford
Norcross, Georgia

Donna Breckenfelder
Wood Dale, Illinois

Jane Breitenbach
Carmichael, California

Teri Brennar
North Branch, Michigan

Nancy Broadley
Ranson, West Virginia

Becki Brown
Wellington, Kansas

Seenie Brown
Port Orchard, Washington

Jacqueline Busacker
Cheyenne, Wyoming

Sharon Butler
Tucumcari, New Mexico

Rose Card
Ferron, Utah

Judy Carlson
Paola, Kansas

Jan Carpenter
LaPorte, Colorado

Pamela Carrier
Berlin, New Hampshire

Linda Carter
Midland, Michigan

Terry Caughern
Heavener, Oklahoma

Augustine Cheatham
Montgomery, Alabama

Jackie Church
Holly, Michigan

Kathy Churchy
Camden, Delaware

Denise Cinnamon
Louisville, Kentucky

Mary Clapp
Norcross, Georgia

Ron Clark
Centerville, Iowa

Amanda Coley
Chattanooga, Tennessee

Susan Colford
Little Rock, Arkansas

Cindy Collins
Skidmore, Missouri

Janet Comfort
Jackson, Wyoming

Kay Conception
Mt. Clemens, Michigan

Lucia Cornwell
Warwick, Rhode Island

Angie Craig
Bloomington, Indiana

Joan Culver
Carmichael, California

Nancy Davis
Palm Bay, Florida

Patsy DeVeau
Corpus Christi, Texas

Sarah Dew
Nichols, South Carolina

Jean Ann Dimick
Helper, Utah

Dianne Ellingson
Baker City, Oregon

Jill Elliott
Marion, North Carolina

Yvonne Ellis
Brooklyn, New York

Necia Erramouspe
Helper, Utah

Theresa Fallwek
Corpus Christi, Texas

June Farber
Broomall, Pennsylvania

Veronica Feehan
Newark, New Jersey

Mary Feltz
Prairie Du Sac, Wisconsin

Michael Ferro
Wheeling, West Virginia

Blanche Flores
Corpus Christi, Texas

Rachel Fluke
Harpers Ferry, West Virginia

Barbara Fontan
Covington, Louisiana
Nancy Fortman
Ottawa, Ohio
Joyce Fowler
Easley, South Carolina
Donna Friesel
Bloomington, Indiana
Patti Fulcher
Canadian, Texas
Marie Fuller
Mounds, Oklahoma
Lise Gagnon
Berlin, New Hampshire
Marleda Gambill
Michigan City, Indiana
Rosario Garcia
Corpus Christi, Texas
Ann Garrett
Mount Vernon, Illinois
Anita Gayheart
Anchorage, Alaska
Constance Gemeny
Sterling, Illinois
Donna Gericke
Sterling, Illinois
Julie Gilmore
Ogden, Utah
Dee Ginn
Wellington, Kansas
Jean Grant
Richmond Hill, Georgia
Jim Greetham
Port Orchard, Washington
Barbara Gump
Little Rock, Arkansas
Paulita Guzman
Mercedes, Texas
Madeline Hammond
East Greenwich, Rhode Island
Louella Hanlin
Wheeling, West Virginia
Sally Hannert
Mt. Clemens, Michigan
Barbara Hanson
Norcross, Georgia

Sarah Hare
Camden, Delaware
Terry Hart
Omaha, Nebraska
Catherine Haslett
Madison Heights, Michigan
Judy Helstrom
Minneapolis, Minnesota
Karen Hermann
West Chester, Pennsylvania
Margarita Hernandez
Mercedes, Texas
Syneva Heupel
Great Falls, Montana
Dody (Batson) Hill
San Carlos, Arizona
Phyllis Holste
Hardin, Illinois
A. Hoover
Hinesville, Georgia
Coella Houser
Helper, Utah
Joanne Hunt
North Las Vegas, Nevada
Pam Hunt
Willoughby, Ohio
Marilyn Isakson
Charles City, Iowa
Bonnie Jacobs
Kansas City, Missouri
Patricia Jaworski
Dorchester, Massachusetts
Chris Jensen
Exira, Iowa
Barbara Johnson
Covington, Louisiana
Mary Ann Jones
Bloomington, Indiana
Neva Jean Jones
Corpus Christi, Texas
Theresa Joray
Seymour, Indiana
Rose Marie Karp
Little Rock, Arkansas
Nancy Karpowitz
Ferron, Utah

Marilyn Katz
Lawrenceville, New Jersey
Clementine Kelley
Little Rock, Arkansas
Deborah Kilander
Portland, Oregon
Susan Kincaid
Richmond Hill, Georgia
Paula Kirkpatrick
East Greenwich, Rhode Island
Suzanne Knott
Ottawa, Ohio
Dianne Kuehl
Prairie Du Sac, Wisconsin
Dean Kuhlman
Kenosha, Wisconsin
Marcia Larson
Great Falls, Montana
Beverly Ledford
Fallston, North Carolina
Ted Lewis
Camden, Delaware
Kathlyn Lindquist
Minneapolis, Minnesota
Barbara Link
Broomall, Pennsylvania
Sandra Lojewski
Willoughby, Ohio
Merna Lowey
Michigan City, Indiana
Consuelo Lozano
Mercedes, Texas
Carrie Manigo
Richmond Hill, Georgia
Barbara Markulik
Englewood, Colorado
Peter Martin
Salt Lake City, Utah
Calvin Matsumura
Pearl City, Hawaii
Gayle Mayfield
Paola, Kansas
Frances Mazzei
East Greenwich, Rhode Island
Judy McCaughey
Warwick, Rhode Island

Debbie McCrum
Berlin, New Hampshire
Nancy McDonald
Richmond Hill, Georgia
Mary McElroy
Cleveland, Ohio
Dianna McGarr
Canadian, Texas
Betsy McGraw
Louisville, Kentucky
Mary Jane McGuire
Carrollton, Missouri
Laurie McLeroy
Norcross, Georgia
Helen Metz
Cheyenne, Wyoming
Terry Moriarty
Pontiac, Michigan
Aileen Moriwake
Aiea, Hawaii
Alia Morrison
Brooklyn, New York
Fran Mortland
Hardin, Illinois
Beverly Newland
Stanfield, Oregon
Barbara Nicholls
Dorchester, Massachusetts
Eunice Niebaum
Great Falls, Montana
Leann Norris
Flat River, Missouri
Marianne O'Rourke
Montour Falls, New York
Mary Ann Oldham
Rexburg, Idaho
Anna Olson
Lakewood, California
Lynn Olson
Barnesville, Minnesota
Dorothy Ondracek
Berwyn, Illinois
Jane Owen
Virginia Beach, Virginia
Valerie Padmore
Witten, South Dakota

Faye Paster
Minneapolis, Minnesota
Terrie Patullo
Manassas, Virginia
Mautha Peeler
York, South Carolina
Esperanza Pemelton
Mercedes, Texas
Nancy Pennington
Leonard, Texas
Kathleen Petersen
Ferron, Utah
Debora Peterson
Helper, Utah
Ralph Peterson
Algonquin, Illinois
Marlisa Pierce
Montgomery, Alabama
Barbara Pool
Marion, North Carolina
Thyla Popejoy
Trumann, Arkansas
Janet Pratt
West Milford, West Virginia
Sandra Ramsay
Trumann, Arkansas
Lori Raveling
Corpus Christi, Texas
Dede Redden
Trumann, Arkansas
Dee Anna Rees
Rexburg, Idaho
Edgar Rehmer
Algonquin, Illinois
Barbara Reichardt
El Monte, California
Terri Reichen
Torrington, Connecticut
Gayle Reid
Shelburne, Vermont
Donna Reynolds
Abilene, Kansas
Cathy Rheinberger
Centerville, Iowa
Lee Ann Roberts
Hazlehurst, Georgia

Varina Roush
Richmond Hill, Georgia
Cheryl Royak
Cleveland, Ohio
Lucille Rugg
Palm Bay, Florida
Toni Sandlin
Newtown Square, Pennsylvania
Lori Saunders
Sterling, Illinois
Melody Schreder
Sidney, Montana
Barbara Smith
Rexburg, Idaho
Roger Schwartz
Clementon, New Jersey
Teresa Sheerin
Ely, Nevada
Cheryl Shulkusky
Harrisburg, Pennsylvania
Marcie Simon
Aiea, Hawaii
Barbara Smith
Rexburg, Idaho
Kay Smith
Bloomington, Indiana
Barbara Snodgrass
Random Lake, Wisconsin
Constance Solheim
Virginia Beach, Virginia
Mrs. Somers
Maple Shade, New Jersey
Harriet Speece
Willoughby, Ohio
Patricia Spelios
Normal, Illinois
Sheila Steadman
Shreveport, Louisiana
Betty Stensrud
Minneapolis, Minnesota
Debra Stepleton
Mountain View, Hawaii
Sue Stiffler
Exira, Iowa
Vicky Stormoe
Fargo, North Dakota

Camla Stout
  Boulder, Montana
Nancy Stowe
  Montgomery, Alabama
Carolyn Strickland
  Hinesville, Georgia
Tonya Stripling
  Little Rock, Arkansas
Amy Stroud
  New Bern, North Carolina
Nancy Stubbs
  Jackson, Mississippi
Janet Sudduth
  Virginia Beach, Virginia
Vicki Suter
  Springfield, Tennessee
Betsy Swartwood
  Long Lake, Minnesota
Nancy Swift
  Random Lake, Wisconsin
Carolyn Tarantine
  Mansfield, Ohio
Calie Torgerson
  North Las Vegas, Nevada
Elaine Tressler
  Willoughby, Ohio
Vicki Tucker
  Norcross, Georgia
Linda Tutunjian
  Newark, New Jersey
Lois Ueland
  Hampstead, New Hampshire
Carol Vedral
  Lawrenceville, New Jersey
Pat Vielhak
  Cheyenne, Wyoming
Delphia Vinnedge
  Kalispell, Montana
Ann Wade
  Indianapolis, Indiana

Lisa Wakely
  Montgomery, Alabama
Kathy Warren
  North Las Vegas, Nevada
Sharon Webber
  Clarence, New York
Gale Weber
  Rexburg, Idaho
Anne Webster
  Jacksonville, Florida
George Weeks
  St. Matthews, South Carolina
Carolyn Weigand
  Circleville, Ohio
Nancy Weir
  Little Rock, Arkansas
Susan Wetmore
  Baker, Nevada
Carol White
  Roxboro, North Carolina
Mamie White
  St. Louis, Missouri
Linda Wiesner
  New Ulm, Minnesota
Cathy Wildman
  Bloomington, Maryland
Sharon Wildman
  Norcross, Georgia
Sandra Williams
  Bethlehem, Pennsylvania
Terry Williams
  Trumann, Arkansas
Beverly Woltkamp
  Lakewood, California
Doris Jean Wood
  Hinesville, Georgia
Cathye Wood
  Englewood, Colorado
Jill Zaterka
  Worcester, Massachusetts

Appendix B:

Fifty-five Error Categories for
Classifying Misspelled Words

Following are the fifty-five categories that were used for classifying misspelled words in Research in Action, with examples of the types of spelling errors that were classified in each error type.

Vowel Errors

1. Long *a* (*age, braid*)
2. Long *e* (*be, complete*)
3. Long *i* (*five, sky*)
4. Long *o* (*open, oak*)
5. /ü/ (*rule, move*)
6. Short *a* (*hat, plaid*)
7. Short *e* (*let, said*)
8. Short *i* (*it, pin*)
9. Short *o* (*hot, watch*)
10. Short *u* (*cup, flood*)
11. /ä/ (*father, heart*)
12. /ô/ (*all, more, bought*)
13. /u̇/ (*full, good*)
14. /oi/ (*boy, voice*)
15. /ou/ (*house, owl*)
16. /yü/ (*few, music*)
17. /ėr/ (*bird, word*)
18. /ə/ final syllable (*middle, angel*)
19. /ə/ others (*favorite*)
20. Silent *e*, long vowel (*rode*)
21. Silent *e*, other (*love, have*)
22. Silent *e*, overgeneralized (*had—hade*)

Consonant Errors

23. Consonant substitution (*cat—kat*)
24. Single consonant, doubled (*city—citty*)
25. Double consonant in root (*little—litle*)
26. Consonant blend (*bump—bup*)
27. Consonant digraph (*patch—pach*)
28. Silent consonant (*wrong—rong*)
29. Complex consonant (*stomach—stomak*)

Word Structure Errors: Affixes

30. Prefix (*misspell—mispell*)
31. Suffix (*nervous—nerves*)
32. *y* to *i* + suffix
    (*happily—happyly*)
33. Final *e* + suffix
    (*argument—arguement*)
34. Doubled consonant
    + suffix (*finally—finaly*)

Word Structure Errors: Inflected Endings

(-ed, -ing, -er, -est, -s, -es)

35. Inflected spelling
    (*looked—lookd*)
36. *y* to *i* + inflected ending
    (*cried—cryed*)
37. Final *e* + inflected ending
    (*posing—poseing*)
38. Double consonant with
    inflected ending
    (*hated—hatted*)

Compound

39. Compound word spelling
    (*everything—everthing*)
40. Compound wrongly
    joined/hyphenated
    (*baby-sit—babysit*)
41. Compound wrongly sepa-
    rated (*outside—out side*)
42. Wrongly run together/sep-
    arated (*because—be cause;
    a lot—alot*)

Usage Convention

43. Capitalization
    (*Iowa—iowa*)
44. Abbreviation (*Feb.—Febre*)
45. Homophone
    (*too—to—two*)
46. Easily confused pairs
    (*where—were*)
47. Regularizing irregulars
    (*ran—runned*)
48. Apostrophe with
    possessive (*mom's—moms*)
49. Apostrophe with
    contraction (*didn't—didnt*)

Twilight Zone Errors

50. Added letters
    (*athlete—athalete*)
51. Omitted letters
    (*probably—probly*)
52. Repeated sequence
    (*remember—rememember*)
53. Scrambled letters
    (*only—olny*)
54. Truncated or bizarre
    (50% or more omitted:
    because—bcz)
55. Mispronunciation
    (*want to—wanna*)

Appendix C:

100 Most Commonly Misspelled
Words at Each Grade, 1–8

Grade 1

because	what	end	school
when	our	pretty	dinosaurs
like	their	sometimes	is
they	nice	I'm	made
went	of	one	much
too	once	other	next
said	I	saw	night
there	some	thank	out
house	that	come	played
know	little	Easter	think
with	then	everybody	wanted
have	to	party	where
very	and	sister	witch
friend	part	but	your
my	for	came	babies
was	favorite	didn't	bird
would	get	girl	funny
are	Mom	good	got
want	birthday	will	teacher
friends	going	always	them
were	her	brother	a lot
people	outside	don't	after
about	the	home	again
Christmas	could	love	around
play	Dad	scared	before

Grade 2

because
too
they
when
there
went
their
Christmas
people
favorite
friends
were
said
our
a lot
would
upon
know
friend
outside
Easter
once
again
didn't
scared

that's
house
Halloween
with
very
baseball
heard
then
what
everybody
I
and
another
little
first
night
sometimes
thought
want
two
about
every
whole
before
could

like
started
to
some
it's
took
special
they're
through
caught
really
other
presents
swimming
where
don't
family
into
them
tried
was
beautiful
brother
different
found

have
knew
nice
one
there's
watch
always
aunt
brought
children
everything
getting
happily
him
second
something
wanted
world
believe
cheese
down
great
haunted
hurt
I'm

Grade 3

too	different	would	swimming
because	they're	brother	very
there	once	could	who
their	until	pretty	back
a lot	where	caught	first
Christmas	before	whole	into
were	presents	morning	school
said	we're	took	stopped
went	and	believe	animals
they	another	his	brought
favorite	sometimes	it's	family
when	didn't	started	let's
friend	heard	beautiful	Mom
know	little	two	about
that's	through	almost	around
upon	off	clothes	bought
with	outside	cousin	friend's
our	something	everything	happily
really	thought	getting	teacher
friends	Halloween	I'm	told
then	people	scared	coming
I	everybody	was	happened
always	want	what	tried
finally	house	everyone	are
again	one	found	girl

Grade 4

too	where	first	before
a lot	caught	watch	doesn't
because	chocolate	people	dollars
there	friend	always	every
their	into	took	found
favorite	everybody	everyone	maybe
that's	off	morning	once
our	through	school	other
when	friends	something	stopped
really	swimming	with	there's
they're	want	would	and
were	you're	are	bought
it's	another	enough	Easter
know	beautiful	except	getting
finally	I'm	friend's	going
again	let's	probably	little
they	then	upon	no
Christmas	believe	vacation	stuff
went	cousin	brought	together
until	especially	house	turned
outside	happened	might	usually
said	heard	myself	against
we're	I	basketball	birthday
sometimes	whole	hospital	break
different	didn't	opened	buy

Grade 5

a lot
too
their
there
because
favorite
that's
finally
our
they're
it's
really
different
where
again
until
friend
they
you're
friends
through
were
believe
know
something

probably
Christmas
to
when
didn't
heard
then
we're
everybody
Mom
everyone
one
went
decided
especially
getting
Halloween
off
always
whole
happened
I'm
into
maybe
said

there's
thought
upon
usually
Dad
knew
sometimes
want
which
caught
let's
stopped
TV
beautiful
before
buy
Dad's
doesn't
everything
except
tried
and
another
clothes
don't

excited
outside
piece
school
field
friend's
myself
since
family
grabbed
once
people
right
should
vacation
weird
what's
already
college
exciting
first
himself
surprised
threw
aren't

Grade 6

a lot
too
it's
because
that's
their
there
you're
favorite
were
everything
finally
our
probably
they're
until
different
really
usually
beautiful
college
they
through
where
we're

again
clothes
didn't
everybody
off
TV
myself
basketball
let's
there's
which
themselves
then
always
awhile
Christmas
doesn't
except
outside
when
whole
beginning
business
don't
elementary

especially
field
Florida
friend
grabbed
since
something
swimming
to
getting
guess
I'm
know
one
want
went
would
and
bored
can't
cousin's
environment
exciting
friends
happened

Hawaii
he's
heard
house
I
I've
into
license
met
no
now
planet
someone
sometimes
started
stopped
than
together
upstairs
wear
what's
wouldn't
anything
anyway
around

Grade 7

there
a lot
too
their
that's
it's
because
don't
probably
they're
Easter
they
you're
finally
our
Christmas
off
where
Halloween
didn't
until
buy
let's
really
then

usually
we're
went
sometimes
through
which
doesn't
favorite
heard
different
everything
again
believe
except
something
were
always
anything
especially
everyone
friends
everywhere
around
everybody
maybe

no
restaurant
Saturday
someone
there's
beautiful
can't
Mom's
outside
thought
whole
without
and
another
basketball
beginning
couldn't
Friday
grabbed
relatives
vacation
wasn't
college
Dad's
downstairs

happened
into
knew
against
awhile
clothes
field
friend's
going to
minutes
morning
people
remember
right
supposed
to
tomorrow
trying
upstairs
what's
backyard
before
caught
coming
cousin's

Grade 8

a lot	going to	maybe	again
too	through	now	anyway
it's	they	wear	awhile
you're	to	business	coming
their	which	since	except
that's	different	were	happened
there	everything	couldn't	heard
they're	believe	downstairs	knew
because	Christmas	families	one
probably	clothes	friend's	separated
don't	I'm	into	thought
we're	no one	lose	tried
finally	our	restaurant	whole
there's	than	what's	about
where	especially	whether	aren't
can't	let's	without	cannot
usually	then	your	Dad's
doesn't	weird	beautiful	decided
really	favorite	definitely	every day
allowed	friends	everyone	everywhere
didn't	know	friend	experience
off	outside	grabbed	Grandma's
TV	always	hear	having
until	beginning	no	myself
something	college	people	nowhere

Appendix D:

Error Categories by Grade Levels and Total Sample

	Primary 1–3	Intermediate 4–6	Upper 7–8	Total Sample
1.	consonant substitution	omitted letters	homophones	omitted letters
2.	omitted letters	homophones	omitted letters	homophones
3.	short *e*	consonant substitution	schwa (other)	consonant substitution
4.	consonant blend	scrambled letters	scrambled letters	scrambled letters
5.	long *e*	schwa (other)	consonant substitution	schwa (other)
6.	schwa (final syllable)	run together/separated	run together/separated	short *e*
7.	scrambled letters	long *e*	apostrophe with contraction	long *e*
8.	homophones	short *e*	compound wrongly separated	schwa (final syllable)
9.	consonant digraph	schwa (final syllable)	long *e*	consonant blend
10.	inflected spelling	compound wrongly separated	short *e*	run together/separated
11.	complex consonant	added letters	schwa (final syllable)	consonant digraph
12.	short *i*	consonant blend	double consonant in root	added letters
13.	schwa (other)	apostrophe with contraction	capitalization	short *i*

Primary 1-3

14. vowel: /ô/
15. added letters
16. double consonant in root
17. long a
18. silent e-overgeneralized
19. silent e-other
20. short u
21. silent e-long vowel
22. long i
23. run together/separated
24. capitalization
25. truncated/bizarre
26. vowel: /er/
27. single consonant doubled
28. compound wrongly separated
29. apostrophe wtih contraction
30. long o
31. compound word spelling
32. vowel: /ou/

Intermediate 4-6

short i
double consonant in root
consonant digraph

inflected spelling
complex consonant
single consonant doubled
capitalization
vowel: /ô/
silent e-overgeneralized

long a
double consonant + inflected end
apostrophe with possessive
silent e-other
compound word spelling

short u

easily confused pairs

long i
suffix spelling
silent e-long vowel

Upper 7-8

short i
consonant digraph
added letters

single consonant doubled
consonant blend
apostrophe with possessive
inflected spelling
complex consonant
double consonant + inflected end

long a
silent e-overgeneralized

vowel: /ô/
compound wrongly joined
easily confused pairs

suffix spelling

compound word spelling

mispronunciation
short u
vowel: /ü/

Total Sample

double consonant in root
inflected spelling
compound wrongly separated
apostrophe with contraction
complex consonant
vowel: /ô/
capitalization
long a
silent e-overgeneralized

single consonant doubled
silent e-other

short u
apostrophe with possessive
long i

silent e-long vowel

double consonant + inflected end
compound word spelling
vowel: /er/
long o

#				
33. short o	long o	double consonant + suffix	easily confused pairs
34. short a	compound wrongly joined	silent e–other	vowel: /ü/
35. silent consonant	vowel: /er/	y to i + inflected ending	suffix spelling
36. vowel: /ü/	mispronunciation	final e + suffix	truncated/bizarre
37. final e + inflected ending	double consonant + suffix	silent consonant	silent consonant
38. double consonant + inflected end	vowel: /ü/	long o	mispronunciation
39. vowel: /ü/	silent consonant	long i	compound wrongly joined
40. mispronunciation	final e + inflected ending	vowel: /er/	final e + inflected ending
41. apostrophe with possessive	y to i + inflected ending	silent e–long vowel	double consonant + suffix
42. easily confused pairs	truncated/bizarre	final e + inflected ending	vowel: /ou/
43. suffix spelling	final e + suffix	regularizing irregulars	y to i + inflected ending
44. vowel: /ä/	short a	truncated/bizarre	short o
45. y to i + inflected ending	vowel: /ou/	short a	short a
46. double consonant + suffix	short o	short o	vowel: /ü/
47. compound wrongly joined	regularized irregulars	vowel: /ou/	final e + suffix
48. regularizing irregulars	vowel: /ü/	vowel: /ä/	regularizing irregulars
49. vowel: /yü/	repeated sequence	vowel: /yü/	vowel: /ä/
50. repeated sequence	vowel: /yü/	prefix spelling	vowel: /yü/
51. vowel: /oi/	vowel: /ä/	vowel: /ü/	repeated sequence
52. final e + suffix	prefix spelling	repeated sequence	prefix spelling
53. y to i + suffix	abbreviation	abbreviation	abbreviation
54. prefix spelling	y to i + suffix	y to i + suffix	vowel: /oi/
55. abbreviation	vowel: /oi	vowel: /oi/	y to i + suffix

Appendix E:
Grade-by-grade Recommended
Spelling Curriculum

These grade-by-grade recommendations for a spelling curriculum are based on the findings of Research in Action (Cramer and Cipielewski, 1995).

Grade 1

Sound Patterns
Short vowels
Long vowels
Common consonant sounds
Common blends
Common digraphs

Developing Spelling Consciousness
Sight words

Structure Rules
Forming plurals with
  -s and -es
Adding -ed and -ing
  (no spelling changes)

Spelling Strategies
Steps for spelling new words

Spelling and Meaning
Not suggested at this grade

Commonly Misspelled Words
Use the Grade 1 list from
Appendix C.

Grade 2

Sound Patterns
Variations in short and long
  vowels
Vowel digraphs
Vowel sounds with *r*
Blends
Digraphs (spelling variations)

Structure Rules
Forming plurals with *-s*
  and *-es*
Adding *-ed* and *-ing*
  • no spelling changes
  • doubling final consonants

Spelling and Meaning
Homophones
Compound words
Contractions

Developing Spelling Consciousness
Including all the letters
Using just enough letters
Getting letters in the right
  order

Spelling Strategies
Steps for spelling new words
Rhyming helpers
Problem parts
Dividing long words

Commonly Misspelled Words
Use the Grade 2 list from
Appendix C.

Grade 3

Sound Patterns

Variations in short and long vowels

Some difficult spellings of other vowel sounds

Variations of common consonant sounds such as /j/, /k/, and /s/

Blends, digraphs, and double consonants

Silent consonants

Developing Spelling Consciousness

Including all the letters

Using just enough letters

Getting letters in the right order

Words with no sound clues (schwas)

Structure Rules

Forming plurals with -s and -es

Adding -ed and -ing
- No spelling changes
- Doubling final consonants
- Changing *y* to *i*
- Dropping final *e*

Adding prefixes and suffixes

Spelling Strategies

Steps for spelling new words

Rhyming helpers

Problem parts

Pronouncing for spelling

Dividing long words

Spelling and Meaning

Homophones

Compound words

Contractions

Commonly Misspelled Words

Use the Grade 3 list from Appendix C.

Grade 4

Sound Patterns

More variations in short and
  long vowels
Additional variations of other
  vowel sounds
Difficult consonant spellings
Less common spellings of
  blends, digraphs, double consonants and silent consonants

Developing Spelling Consciousness

Including all the letters
Using just enough letters
Getting letters in the right
  order
Words with no sound clues
  (schwas)

Structure Rules

Forming plurals with -s
  and -es
Adding -ed, -ing, -er, and -est
  • No spelling changes
  • Doubling final consonants
  • Changing y to i
  • Dropping final e
Adding prefixes and suffixes

Spelling Strategies

Steps for spelling new words
Rhyming helpers
Problem parts
Pronouncing for spelling
Dividing Long words
Choosing the best strategy

Spelling and Meaning

Homophones
Compound words
Contractions
Easily confused words
Related words

Commonly Misspelled Words

Use the Grade 4 list from
  Appendix C.

Grade 5

Sound Patterns
More variations in short and
   long vowels
Additional variations of other
   vowel sounds
More difficult consonant
   spellings
Less common spellings of
   blends, digraphs, double
   consonants and silent
   consonants

Structure Rules
Forming plurals with -s
   and -es
Adding -ed, -ing, -er, and -est
 • No spelling changes
 • Doubling final consonants
 • Changing y to i
 • Dropping final e
Adding prefixes and suffixes

Spelling and Meaning
Homophones
Compound words
Contractions
Easily confused words
Related words

Developing Spelling Consciousness
Including all the letters
Using just enough letters
Getting letters in the right
   order
Words with no sound clues
   (schwas)

Spelling Strategies
Steps for spelling new words
Problem parts
Pronouncing for spelling
Meaning helpers
Memory tricks
Divide and conquer
Choosing the best strategy

Commonly Misspelled Words
Use the Grade 5 list from
   Appendix C.

Grade 6

Sound Patterns
Vowel patterns that cause
  problems (such as *ei* and *ie*)
Unusual vowel spellings
Unusual digraph spellings
  (/sh/ spelled *ti, ci*, etc.)
Unusual consonant spellings

Developing Spelling Consciousness
Including all the letters
Using just enough letters
Getting letters in the right
  order
Words with no sound clues
  (schwas)
Writing one word or two?

Structure Rules
Forming plurals with *-s*
  and *-es*
Irregular plurals:
• Words that end in *f, fe, ff,*
  and *ffe*
• Words that end in *o*
Adding *-ed, -ing, -er,* and *-est*
• No spelling changes
• Doubling final consonants
• Changing *y* to *i*
• Dropping final *e*
Adding prefixes and suffixes

Spelling Strategies
Steps for spelling new words
Problem parts
Pronouncing for spelling
Meaning helpers
Memory tricks
Divide and conquer
Choosing the best strategy

Spelling and Meaning
Homophones
Compound words
Contractions
Easily confused words
Related words

Commonly Misspelled Words
Use the Grade 6 list from
  Appendix C.

Grade 7

Sound Patterns
Unusual or difficult vowel
  spellings
Unusual or difficult consonant spellings

Developing Spelling Consciousness
Including all the letters
Using just enough letters
Getting letters in the right
  order
Words with no sound clues
  (schwas)
Writing one word or two?

Structure Rules
Regular plurals
Irregular plurals:
  • Words that end in *f, fe, ff,*
    and *ffe*
  • Words that end in *o*
  • Words in a new form:
    datum—data
Adding *-ed, -ing, -er,* and *-est*
  • No spelling changes
  • Doubling final consonants
  • Changing *y* to *i*
  • Dropping final *e*
Adding prefixes and suffixes

Spelling Strategies
Steps for spelling new words
Problem parts
Pronouncing for spelling
Meaning helpers
Memory tricks
Divide and conquer
Choosing the best strategy

Spelling and Meaning
Homophones
Apostrophes—possessives and
  contractions
Compound words
Easily confused words
Meaning related words
  • Related words
  • Greek and Latin roots

Commonly Misspelled Words
Use the Grade 7 list from
  Appendix C.

Grade 8

Sound Patterns
Unusual or difficult vowel
  spellings
Unusual or difficult consonant spellings

Developing Spelling Consciousness
Including all the letters
Using just enough letters
Getting letters in the right
  order
Words with no sound clues
  (schwas)
Writing one word or two?

Structure Rules
Regular plurals
Irregular plurals:
- Words that end in *f, fe, ff,*
  and *ffe*
- Words that end in *o*
- Words in a new form:
  datum—data
Adding *-ed, -ing, -er,* and *-est*
- No spelling changes
- Doubling final consonants
- Changing *y* to *i*
- Dropping final *e*
Adding prefixes and suffixes

Spelling Strategies
Steps for spelling new words
Problem parts
Pronouncing for spelling
Meaning helpers
Memory tricks
Divide and conquer
Choosing the best strategy

Spelling and Meaning
Homophones
Apostrophes—possessives and
  contractions
Compound words
Easily confused words
Meaning Related Words
- Related words
- Greek and Latin Roots

Commonly Misspelled Words
Use the Grade 8 list from
  Appendix C.

Appendix F:
Sources for List Words

Commonly Misspelled Words

Spelling research and information: An overview of current research and practices. 1995. Appendix C. Glenview, Ill.: Scott, Foresman, and Company.

This source provides the one hundred words most frequently misspelled by children at each grade level, 1–8, whose compositions were submitted for the Research in Action spelling study.

High Frequency Words

Carroll J. B., P. Davies, and B. Richman. 1971 *American Heritage word frequency book.* Boston: Houghton Mifflin.

This frequency list is based on the frequency with which words occur in printed materials for children; you may want to concentrate on the first 1000 words, which make up almost 90% our written language.

Dolch, E. 1936. A basic sight vocabulary. *Elementary School Journal,* 456–460.

A classic list of 220 words that children need to know.

Harris, A. J., and M. D. Jacobson. 1982. *Basic reading vocabularies.* New York: Macmillan Publishing Co., Inc.

This publication provides an analysis of grade levels at which words are first introduced in text materials published for children.

Word Lists Organized by Sound Patterns

Fry, E. B., and others. 1993. *The reading teacher's book of lists,* 3rd ed. Englewood Cliffs, N.J.:Prentice-Hall, Inc.

Phonics section provides English sounds and lists of words with their common spellings.

Henderson, E. H. 1990. *Teaching spelling,* rev. ed. Boston: Houghton Mifflin.

Probably the most comprehensive source, this book includes an appendix of common English spelling patterns for most vowel and consonant sounds. Also includes lists of homophones, compound words, and related words.

Stahl, S. A. 1992. Say the "p" word: Nine guidelines for exemplary phonics instruction. *The Reading Teacher* 45:618-625.

This is a good starting place if you need to justify phonics instruction in your classroom.

References

Abouzeid, M. 1986. Developmental stages of word knowledge in dyslexia. Ph.D. diss., University of Virginia, Charlottesville.

Adams, M. J. 1990. *Beginning to read: Thinking and learning about print.* Cambridge, Mass.: The M.I.T. Press.

Ayres, L. 1993. The efficacy of three training conditions on phonological awareness of kindergarten children and the longitudinal effect of each on later reading acquisition. Ph.D. diss., Oakland University, Rochester, Michigan.

Ball, E. W., and B. A. Blachman. 1991. Does phoneme awareness training in kindergarten make a difference in early word recognition and spelling development? *Reading Research Quarterly* 26:49–66.

Barnes, W. G. W. 1982. The developmental acquisition of silent letters and orthographic images in English spelling. Ph.D. diss., University of Virginia, Charlottesville.

Bear, D. 1982. Patterns of oral reading across stages of word knowledge. Ph.D. diss., University of Virginia, Charlottesville.

Beers C., and J. Beers. 1980. Vowel spelling strategies among first and second graders: A growing awareness of written words. *Language Arts* 57:166–172.

———. 1981. Three assumptions about learning to spell. *Language Arts* 58:573–580.

———. 1991. Children's knowledge of inflected morphology in spelling. In *Development of orthographic knowledge and the foundations of literacy: A memorial festschrift for Edmund H. Henderson,* edited by S. Templeton and D. Bear. Hillsdale, N.J.: Lawrence Erlbaum Associates.

———. 1991. Understanding children's spelling. In *Spelling Links,* edited by David Booth. Portsmouth, N.H.: Heinemann Educational Books.

Beers, J. 1980. Developmental strategies of spelling competence in primary school children. In *Developmental and cognitive aspects of learning to spell,* edited by J. Beers and E. Henderson. Newark, Del.: International Reading Association, 36–45.

Beers, J. W., and E. H. Henderson. 1977. A study of developing orthographic concepts among first graders. *Research in the Teaching of English* 11:133–148.

Betts, E. A. 1945. Inter-relationship of reading and spelling. *Elementary English Review* 22:12–23.

Bissex, G. 1980. *GYNS AT WRK: A child learns to write and read.* Cambridge, Mass.: Harvard University Press.

Blachman, B. A. 1984. Language analysis skills and early reading acquisition. In *Language learning disabilities in school age children*, edited by G. Wallach and K. Butler, 271–287. Baltimore, M.D.: Williams and Wilkins.

Bradley, L., and P. E. Bryant. 1983. Categorizing sounds and learning to read: A causal connection. *Nature* 30:419–421.

Brown A. L., and A. S. Palinscar. 1982. Inducting strategic learning from texts by means of informed self-control training. Technical Report No. 262, Bethesda, MD: National Institute of Child Health and Human Development.

Buchanan, E. 1989. *Spelling for the whole language classroom.* Winnipeg, Canada: Whole Language Consultants.

Calkins, L. M. 1986. *The art of teaching writing.* Portsmouth, N.H.: Heinemann.

Carroll, J. B., P. Davies, and B. Richman. 1971. *American Heritage word frequency book.* Boston: Houghton Mifflin.

Chomsky, C. 1971. Write first, read later. *Childhood Education* 47:269–299.

———. 1979. Approaching reading through invented spelling. In *Theory and practice of early reading*, edited by L. Resnick and P. Weaver. Hillsdale, N.J.: Lawrence Earlbaum Associates.

Chomsky, N. 1965. *Aspects of the theory of syntax.* Cambridge, Mass.: M.I.T. Press.

———. 1970. Phonology and reading. In *Basic studies on reading*, edited by H. Levin and J. P. Williams. New York: Basic Books.

Chomsky, N., and M. Halle. 1968. *The sound pattern of English.* New York: Harper and Row.

Church, S. M. 1994. Is whole language really warm and fuzzy? *The Reading Teacher* 47 (February) 362–370.

Clarke, L. K. 1989. Encouraging invented spelling in first graders' writings: Effects on learning to spell and read. *Research in the Teaching of English* 22:281–309.

Cramer, B. B. 1985. The effects of writing with invented spelling on general linguistic awareness and phonemic segmentation ability in kindergartners. Ph.D. diss., Oakland University, Rochester, Michigan.

Cramer, R. L. 1968. An investigation of the spelling achievement of two groups of first grade classes on phonologically regular and irregular words and in written composition. Ph.D. diss., University of Delaware, Newark, Delaware.

———. 1970. An investigation of first-grade spelling achievement. *Elementary English* 47 (February) 230–237.

———. 1995. Making better spellers: Integrating spelling, reading, and writing. In *Spelling research and information: An overview of current research and practices.* Glenview, Ill.: Scott, Foresman and Company.

Cramer, R. L., and J. Cipielewski. 1995. Research in action: A study of spelling errors in 18,599 written compositions of children in grades 1–8. In *Spelling research and information: An overview of current research and practices.* Glenview, Ill.: Scott, Foresman and Company.

Cunningham, P., and R. Allington. 1994. *Classrooms that work: They can all read and write.* New York: Harper Collins College Publishers.

DeHaven, E. 1988. *Teaching and learning the language arts,* 3rd ed. Glenview, Ill: Scott, Foresman and Company.

Dobson, L. 1989. Connections in learning to write and read. In *Reading and writing connections,* edited by J. Mason. Needham Heights, Mass.: Allyn and Bacon.

Ehri, L. 1984. How orthography alters spoken language competencies in children learning to read and spell. In *Language awareness and learning to read,* edited by J. Downing and R. Valtin. New York: Springer-Verlag.

Ehri, L., and L. Wilce. 1987. Does learning to spell help beginners learn to read words? *Reading Research Quarterly* 12:47–65.

Gates, A. I. 1936. *Generalization and transfer in spelling.* New York: Bureau of Publications, Teachers College, Columbia University.

Gentry, R. 1977. A study of the orthographic strategies of beginning readers. Ph.D. diss., University of Virginia, Charlottesville.

———. 1987. *Spel . . . is a four-letter word.* Portsmouth, N. H.: Heinemann.

Gentry, R., and J. W. Gillet. 1993. *Teaching kids to spell.* Portsmouth N.H.; Heinemann.

Gill, J. T. 1992. The relationship between word recognition and spelling. In *Development of orthographic knowledge and the foundations of literacy: A memorial festschrift for Edmund H. Henderson,* edited by S. Templeton and D. R. Bear. Hillsdale, N.J.: Lawrence Erlbaum Associates.

Goodman, K. 1976. Reading: A psycholinguistic guessing game. In *Theoretical models and processes of reading,* edited by H. Singer and R. B. Ruddell. Newark, Del.: International Reading Association.

———. 1986. *What's whole in whole language?* Portsmouth, N.H.: Heinemann.

Graham, S., and L. Miller. 1982. Spelling research and practice: A unified approach. In *Spelling,* edited by W. Barbe, A. Francis, and L. Braun. Columbus, Ohio: Zaner-Bloser.

Graves, D. M. 1983. *Writing: Teachers and children at work.* Portsmouth, N.H.: Heinemann.

Hanna, P. R., and J. T. Moore, Jr. 1953. Spelling—from spoken word to written symbol. *Elementary School Journal* 53 (February) 329–337.

Hanna, P. R., J. S. Hanna, R. E. Hodges, and E. H. Rudorf. 1966. Phoneme-grapheme correspondence as cues to spelling improvement. United States Office of Education Cooperative Research, Project No. 1991.

Hanna, P. R., R. E. Hodges., and J. S. Hanna. 1982. The alphabetic base of spelling. In *Spelling,* edited by W. Barbe, A. Francis, and L. Braun. Columbus, Ohio: Zaner-Bloser.

Henderson, E. H. 1989. *Teaching spelling.* Boston: Houghton Mifflin Co.

Henderson, E. H., and J. W. Beers. 1980. *Developmental and cognitive aspects of learning to spell: A reflection of word knowledge.* Newark, Del.: International Reading Association.

Henderson, E. H., and S. Templeton. 1986. A developmental perspective of formal spelling instruction through alphabet, pattern, and meaning. *Elementary School Journal* 86 (3):305–316.

Hodges, R. 1964. A short history of spelling reform in the United States. *Phi Delta Kappan* 45:330–332.

Horn, E. 1960. Spelling. In *The encyclopedia of educational research,* 3d ed. New York: Macmillan Publishing Co.

Horn, T. D. 1947. The effects of the corrected test on learning to spell. *Elementary School Journal* 47 (January) 277–285.

Housel, D. K. 1989. The effects of the writing to read program and invented spelling in kindergarten on phonemic awareness and later reading ability. Ph.D. diss., Oakland University, Rochester, Michigan.

Invernizzi, M. A. 1992. The vowel and what follows: A phonological frame of orthographic analysis. In *Development of orthographic knowledge and the foundations of literacy: A memorial festschrift for Edmund H. Henderson,* edited by S. Templeton and D. R. Bear. Hillsdale, N.J.: Lawrence Erlbaum Associates.

Juel, C., P. Griffith, and P. B. Gough. 1986. Acquisition of literacy: A longitudinal study of children in first and second grade. *Journal of Educational Psychology* 87:243–255.

Mann, V. A., and I. Y. Liberman. 1984. Phonological awareness and verbal short-term memory: Can they presage early reading problems? *Journal of Learning Disabilities* 17:592–599.

Mann, V. A., P. Tobin, and R. Wilson. 1988. Measuring phonological awareness through the invented spelling of kindergarten children. In *Children's reading and the development of phonological awareness,* edited by K. E. Stanovich. Detroit, Mich.: Wayne State University Press.

Masonheimer, P., P. Drum, and L. Ehri. 1984. Does environmental print identification lead children into word reading? *Journal of Reading Behavior* 16: 257–271.

Mencken, H. L. 1941. *The American language: An inquiry into the development of English in the United States.* New York: Alfred A. Knopf.

Moffett, J., and B. J. Wagner. 1976. *Student-centered language arts and reading: K–13. A handbook for teachers,* 2d ed. Boston: Houghton Mifflin Co.

Moriarty, T. 1990. Using children's literature: How literature-based writing influences the development of phonological awareness. Ph.D. diss., Oakland University, Rochester, Michigan.

Morris, D. 1981. Concept of word: A developmental phenomenon in the beginning reading and writing processes. *Language Arts* 58:659–668.

Morris, D., and J. Perney. 1984. Developmental spelling as a predictor of first grade achievement. *The Elementary School Journal* 84:441–457.

Morris, R. 1980. Beginning readers' concept of word. In *Developmental and cognitive aspects of learning to spell*, edited by E. H. Henderson and J. Beers. Newark: Del.: International Reading Association.

Morrison, I. E., and I. F. Perry. 1959. Spelling and reading relationships with incidence of retardation and acceleration. *Journal of Educational Research* 53:222–227.

Pinker, S. 1994. *The language instinct.* New York: William Morrow and Co.

Plessas, G. P., and D. M. Ladley. 1963. Spelling ability and poor reading. *Elementary School Journal* 63:404–408.

Read, C. 1970. Children's perceptions of the sounds of English: Phonology from three to six. Ph.D. diss., Harvard University.

————. 1971. Preschool children's knowledge of English phonology. Harvard Education Review 41:1–34.

————. 1975. Children's categorization of speech sounds in English. NCTE Research Report No. 17, Urbana, Ill.: National Council of Teachers of English.

Rudisell, M. P. 1957. Interrelations of functional phonic knowledge, reading, spelling, and mental age. *Elementary School Journal* 57:267–274.

Rudorf, E. H. 1964. The development of an algorithm for American-English spelling. Ph.D. diss., Stanford University.

Schlagal, R. C. 1982. A qualitative inventory of word knowledge: A cross-sectional study of spelling, grade one to six. Ph.D. diss., University of Virginia, Charlottesville.

Stanovich, K. E. 1988. *Children's reading and the development of phonological awareness.* Detroit, Mich.: Wayne State University Press.

―――. 1994. Romance and reality. *The Reading Teacher* 47, (December/January) 280–291.

Stanovich, K. E., A. E. Cunningham, and B. B. Cramer. 1984. Assessing phonological awareness in kindergarten children: Issues of task comparability. *Journal of Experimental Child Psychology* 38:175–190.

Stauffer R., and W. D. Hammond. 1965. Effectiveness of language arts and basic reader approach to first-grade instruction. Cooperative Research Project 2679 United States Office of Education, Newark, Del., University of Delaware.

―――. 1969. The effectiveness of a language arts and basic reader approach to first grade reading instruction extended into third grade. *The Reading Research Quarterly* 4:469–499

Stauffer, R., W. D. Hammond, W. Oehlkers, and A. Houseman. 1972. Effectiveness of a language arts and basic reader approach to first grade reading instruction extended into sixth grade. Cooperative Research Project 3276, University of Delaware, Newark, Delaware.

Sulzby, E., J. Barnhart, and J. Hieshima. 1989. Forms of writing and rereading from writing. In *Reading and writing connections,* edited by J. Mason. Needham Heights, Mass.: Allyn and Bacon.

Temple, C. 1978. An analysis of spelling errors in Spanish. Ph.D. diss., University of Virginia, Charlottesville.

Templeton, S. 1976. An awareness of certain aspects of derivational morphology in phonology and orthography among sixth, eighth, and tenth graders. Ph.D. diss., University of Virginia, Charlottesville.

———. 1980. Spelling, phonology and the older student. In *Developmental and cognitive aspects of learning to spell,* edited by E. Henderson and J. Beers. Newark, Del.: International Reading Association,.

———. 1983. Using the spelling/meaning connection to develop word knowledge in older students. *Journal of Reading* 27:8–15.

———. 1989. Tacit and explicit knowledge of derivational morphology: Foundations for a unified approach to spelling and vocabulary development in the intermediate grades and beyond. *Reading Psychology* 10:3.

———. 1992. Theory, nature, and pedagogy of higher-order orthographic development in older students. In *Development of orthographic knowledge and foundations of literacy: A memorial festschrift for Edmund H. Henderson,* edited by S. Templeton and D. Bear. Hillsdale, N.J.: Lawrence Erlbaum Associates.

Templeton, S., and D. Barone. 1989. Explicit awareness of derivational morphological relationships in English orthography. Unpublished manuscript, University of Nevada, Reno, Nevada.

Templeton, S., and D. R. Bear, eds. 1992. *Development of orthographic knowledge and the foundations of literacy: A memorial festschrift for Edmund H. Henderson.* Hillsdale, N.J.: Lawrence Erlbaum Associates.

Templin, M. C. 1954. Phonetic knowledge and its relation to the spelling and reading achievement of fourth grade pupils. *Journal of Educational Research* 45:441–454.

Thomas, V. 1979. *Teaching spelling,* 2d ed. Toronto: Gage Publishing.

Venezky, R. 1970. *The structure of English orthography.* The Hague, Netherlands: Mouton.

Venezky, R. L., and R. H. Weir. 1966. A study of selected spelling-to-sound correspondence patterns. Cooperative Research Project Number 3090, Stanford University.

Wing, A. M., and A. D. Baddeley. 1980. Spelling errors in handwriting: A corpus and a distributional analysis. In *Cognitive Processes in Spelling,* edited by U. Frith. New York: Academic Press.

Zutell, J. 1979. Spelling strategies of primary school children and their relationship to Piaget's concept of decentration. *Research in the Teaching of English* 13:69–80.